"No effort is more dear to my heart than Christ-centered preaching—and no p......
has been more valiant in the cause than Edmund Clowney. This collection of sermons
reflecting his principles includes messages I have my students read, and it will be a sure
blessing to many more."
—Bryan Chapell, President, Covenant Theological Seminary (PCA)

"Our churches desperately need Christ-centered preaching today. But how do we preach
in a way that exalts Christ? How can we preach Christ and still give sermons that speak
to the hearts of those who hear us? What a wonderful gift, therefore, to read sermons
from gifted and experienced pastors where Christ is proclaimed. Often we learn most
effectively by watching experts at work. The passion of Edmund P. Clowney lives on in
the sermons of his students, and what a joy it would bring him to see Christ glorified by
a new generation of preachers."
—Thomas R. Schreiner, James Buchanan Harrison Professor of New Testament
Interpretation, The Southern Baptist Theological Seminary

"I can think of no list of contributors who could better honor the work and legacy of
Edmund Clowney than those who have been brought together in this volume. Their
skills at understanding and interpreting the presence of the grace of Christ in all of the
Scripture serve as both model and encouragement to all whose calling and task it is to
open God's Word to God's people."
—Robert M. Norris, Pastor, Fourth Presbyterian Church, Bethesda, MD

"Edmund Clowney was one of my most valued friends and mentors and perhaps my
very favorite preacher. Ed advocated and exemplified what is called the *redemptive-
historical* approach to preaching. Although I have had some reservations about the *theory*
of redemptive-historical preaching, Ed's sermons moved my heart more than most any
others. For his preaching was not just the application of a theory; it was born out of his
love for Christ and his passion to bring Christ to people and they to him. Others have
advocated the same theory, but only a few have captured Ed's passion, his heart and
soul. And only a few have shared Ed's great gifts of knowledge, clarity, persuasiveness,
and understanding of human nature. Many of those are here, in this volume. May God
use this book to raise up a new generation of preachers filled with his Spirit, to honor
his Son, and may he use it to raise up Christians who passionately embrace God's grace
and share it with others."
—John Frame, Professor of Systematic Theology and Philosophy,
Reformed Theological Seminary

"Edmund Clowney made a significant impact on the revival of biblical theology
in preaching that cannot be assessed from his writings alone. Here we are given an
insight into this impact on a number of his students who pay tribute to his spiritual and
practical influence. It is a rare treat for all of us who value Christ-centered preaching. This
collection of sermons, each prefaced with a statement of the preacher's own estimate
of Clowney's influence as a teacher, provides us with clear hands-on evidence for the
richness of preaching that is informed by Clowney's perspective on biblical theology.
This is a volume that will encourage and inform those who desire to preach Christ from
the whole Bible."
—Graeme Goldsworthy, Visiting Lecturer in Hermeneutics,
Moore Theological College, Sydney, Australia

HERALDS
OF THE
KING

CHRIST-CENTERED SERMONS
IN THE TRADITION OF
EDMUND P. CLOWNEY

EDITED BY DENNIS E. JOHNSON

CROSSWAY BOOKS
WHEATON, ILLINOIS

Heralds of the King: Christ-Centered Sermons in the Tradition of Edmund P. Clowney

Copyright © 2009 by the Edmund P. Clowney Legacy Corporation
Published by Crossway Books
        a publishing ministry of Good News Publishers
        1300 Crescent Street
        Wheaton, Illinois 60187

Design and typesetting by Lakeside Design Plus
Cover design: Cindy Kiple
First printing 2009

Printed in the United States of America

Scripture quotations from the American Standard Version of the Bible.

Scripture quotations from the *ESV® Bible (Holy Bible, English Standard Version®)*, copyright © 2001 by Crossway Bibles, a publishing ministry of Good News Publishers. Used by permission. All rights reserved.

Scripture quotations from the *King James Version* of the Bible.

Scripture quotations from *The Holy Bible: New International Version®*. Copyright © 1973, 1978, 1984 by International Bible Society. Used by permission of Zondervan Publishing House. All rights reserved.

The "NIV" and "New International Version" trademarks are registered in the United States Patent and Trademark Office by International Bible Society. Use of either trademark requires the permission of International Bible Society.

Scripture quotations from *The New King James Version*. Copyright © 1982, Thomas Nelson, Inc. Used by permission.

Scripture quotations from the Holman Christian Standard Bible®. Copyright © 2003, 2002, 2000, 1999 by Holman Bible Publishers. All rights reserved.

All emphases in Scripture quotations have been added.

Timothy J. Keller, "The Girl Nobody Wanted" is © Timothy J. Keller and used by permission.

Trade Paperback ISBN: 978-1-4335-0402-0
PDF ISBN: 978-1-4335-1243-8
Mobipocket ISBN: 978-1-4335-1244-5

Library of Congress Cataloging-in-Publication Data
Heralds of the king : Christ-centered sermons in the tradition of Edmund P. Clowney / edited by Dennis E. Johnson.
        p. cm.
    Includes bibliographical references and index.
    ISBN 978-1-4335-0402-0 (tpb)
    1. Reformed church—Sermons. 2. Sermons, American. I. Clowney, Edmund P. II. Johnson, Dennis E. (Dennis Edward) III. Title.
    BX9495.H47 2009
    252'.05—dc22   2008044150

VP		17	16	15	14	13	12	11	10	09
		9	8	7	6	5	4	3	2	1

In Memory of

Edmund Prosper Clowney
(1917–2005)
and
Jean Wright Clowney
(1920–2008)

CONTENTS

PREFACE

This is a gift from preachers to preachers, and to all God's children who gather, Sunday by Sunday, hungry and thirsty to hear afresh their Father's declaration of love for them and triumph over their enemies through Jesus, his beloved Son. Its development has been our labor of love for two persons: *first, proximately*, for our dear (and sometimes daunting) teacher, mentor, and model, Dr. Edmund P. Clowney, through whom each of the contributors, at various points in our Christian pilgrimage, became captivated in wonder over the glory and grace of Jesus the Christ. Jesus is that *second, supremely* worthy Person whom we love, to whom we offer these efforts to proclaim his Word as our thank offering, first for his saving grace and then for his gifts to his church, including a pastor and teacher such as Ed Clowney. We love because Christ first loved us and gave his life to make us his own. As you will discover in the introductions to the sermons, each of us whose paths crossed Ed's realize how much he would want this little book to deflect attention away from himself and instead to rivet our admiring gaze solely on the Savior. He would be particularly pleased, I suspect, that our publisher insisted on inserting "Christ-centered" in the original subtitle that I had first proposed, so that "Christ" comes before "Clowney" there, as he should everywhere!

Our aim is twofold: first, we are eager to share with you the burning passion to preach Christ from all of Scripture, which we "caught" from Ed. As you will see, this infectious eagerness to attune our ears to hear the Holy Spirit's witness to the Son in every text of the Bible, from every era of redemptive history, was something that we contracted not only from Ed the homiletician or Ed the exegete and biblical theologian, but also from Ed the sinner saved by divine grace, who himself stood amazed and humbled at the mercy shown him at Christ's cross. As you read the chapter introductions, each composed without reading the others, you will be impressed by the consistency of our impressions of Ed's humility and contagious wonder at the glory of Christ radiating from every page of God's Word. Perhaps most striking are the testimonies of students from different generations at different institutions who found themselves so overwhelmed in worship as Ed opened the Word in the classroom that they could not take notes on the lecture-turned-paean-of-praise.

We cannot now take you back with us into a seminary classroom or church sanctuary, to share precisely our experience of "burning hearts" (Luke 24:32) as we were led in the discovery of the Christ who suffered and entered into glory throughout the Scriptures. As of March 20, 2005, Ed stands before the throne of the Lamb, singing the praises of the singing Savior whose grace he had preached to struggling sinners on earth for more than sixty years. (You can, however, hear almost one hundred of Dr. Clowney's sermons and lectures online through the audio collection that has been assembled by the Edmund P. Clowney Legacy Corporation at http://www.sermonaudio.com/source_detail.asp?sourceid=epclegacy.) We hope that our introductions to the sermons will give readers a taste of the person that Ed was (by grace alone, he would always insist!), thereby reinforcing the point that preaching Christ from all the Scriptures is not an automatic product of an abstract hermeneutic method (though it entails sound interpretive principles and practices) but rather grows from a heart that feasts daily in fellowship with the Savior through his Word.

Our second purpose is to show that *one does not have to be Ed Clowney* to see Christ revealed on every page of Scripture and to broadcast the good news of his redemptive achievement in your own ministry, whether your calling is that of a pastor charged to shepherd God's flock or that of one bearing informal witness among family, friends, and coworkers. This case is easier to make today than it was in 1952, when Ed transitioned from pastoral ministry into teaching practical theology at Westminster Theological Seminary.

It was almost a half century ago that his *Preaching and Biblical Theology* appeared.[1] That slight (121 pages) but groundbreaking volume, the first that Ed wrote for publication,[2] engaged issues raised by the "Biblical Theology" movement then current in historical-critical circles, and it touched on the pre-World War II debate in the Netherlands over redemptive-historical versus "exemplary" preaching. Ed harvested the rich legacy of Reformed covenant theology, of Protestant predecessors in the sober exploration of biblical typology such as Patrick Fairbairn, and especially of Geerhardus Vos's insights into the implications of the fact that God embedded his written Word into the unfolding of his plan of redemption in history. Affirming the unity of God's redemptive deeds in history and his inerrant words in Scripture, which attests and interprets those deeds, Ed mapped a homiletic that draws its authority from the God who speaks and saves, its content from the whole Bible (in its temporal, thematic, and formal diversity as well as its theological, christocentric unity), its vividness from a sensitivity to the dramatic, flesh-and-blood concreteness of God's engagement in Israel's and our struggles, and its motivating power from the savoring of divine grace that transcends our wildest imagination.

Preaching and Biblical Theology would eventually be followed, when Ed's responsibilities as seminary president and professor abated somewhat and his service to the church permitted, by other contributions on the theme of Christ-centered preaching, informed by Scripture's redemptive-historical character: "Preaching Christ from All the Scriptures" in the anthology *The Preacher and Preaching* (1986), *The Unfolding Mystery: Discovering Christ in the Old Testament* (1988), *Preaching Christ in All of Scripture* (2003), and *How Jesus Transforms the Ten Commandments* (2007).[3] Less visible

---

1. Edmund P. Clowney, *Preaching and Biblical Theology* (Grand Rapids, MI: Eerdmans, 1961; London: Tyndale, 1962).

2. Edmund P. Clowney, *Eutychus (and His Pin)* (Grand Rapids, MI: Eerdmans, 1960) appeared the previous year, but it was a collection of articles originally written for the periodical *Christianity Today*.

3. Samuel T. Logan Jr., ed., *The Preacher and Preaching: Reviving the Art in the Twentieth Century* (Phillipsburg, NJ: Presbyterian & Reformed, 1986); Edmund P. Clowney, *The Unfolding*

on his résumé but probably more influential for the progress of the gospel and the health of Christ's church have been the hundreds of pastors—heralds of the King—whose hearts have been set on fire by Ed's example in the pulpit and whose minds have been honed by his incisive coaching and critique in the Homiletics classroom.

Today others are catching the vision and passing the spark along, both in pulpit and in print. Some have been Ed's students or colleagues in person: for example, Charlie Drew, one of our contributors, has authored *The Ancient Love Song: Finding Christ in the Old Testament* to lead thoughtful Christians along the paths by which God drew his people in hope and longing toward their ultimate Champion and true Husband.[4] Iain Duguid, another contributor, has explored the Old Testament's witness to Christ in such studies as *Living in the Gap between Promise and Reality: The Gospel according to Abraham*; and in *Hero of Heroes*, he has set Jesus' Beatitudes in the context of our Lord's self-disclosure, showing that these "blessings," too often experienced either as sentimental idealism or as guilt-imposing impossibilities, in fact point our hearts toward the Blessed Hero who inaugurated God's kingdom through his innocent suffering and victorious resurrection.[5]

Other homileticians who are advocating Christ-centered preaching informed by Scripture's redemptive-historical structure have not been Ed's students or associates, but they give evidence of acquaintance with his thought. These include Bryan Chapell, Sidney Greidanus, and Graeme Goldsworthy.[6] Series such as *The Gospel in the Old Testament*[7] and the *Reformed Expository Commentary*[8]

Mystery: Discovering Christ in the Old Testament (Colorado Springs: NavPress, 1988); Clowney, *Preaching Christ in All of Scripture* (Wheaton, IL: Crossway, 2003); Clowney, *How Jesus Transforms the Ten Commandments* (Phillipsburg, NJ: P&R, 2007).

4. Charles D. Drew, *The Ancient Love Song: Finding Christ in the Old Testament* (Phillipsburg, NJ: P&R, 2000).

5. Iain M. Duguid, *Living in the Gap between Promise and Reality: The Gospel according to Abraham* (Phillipsburg, NJ: P&R, 1999). Duguid, *Hero of Heroes: Seeing Christ in the Beatitudes* (Phillipsburg, NJ: P&R, 2001).

6. For example, Bryan Chapell, *Christ-Centered Preaching: Redeeming the Expository Sermon* (2nd ed., Grand Rapids, MI: Baker, 2005); Sidney Greidanus, *Preaching Christ from the Old Testament: A Contemporary Hermeneutical Method* (Grand Rapids, MI: Eerdmans, 1999); Greidanus, *Preaching Christ from Ecclesiastes: Foundations for Expository Sermons* (Grand Rapids: Eerdmans, forthcoming); Graeme Goldsworthy, *Preaching the Whole Bible as Christian Scripture: The Application of Biblical Theology to Expository Preaching* (Grand Rapids, MI: Eerdmans, 2000).

7. Raymond B. Dillard, *Faith in the Face of Apostasy: The Gospel according to Elijah and Elisha* (Phillipsburg, NJ: P&R, 1999) and later volumes.

8. Philip G. Ryken, *Galatians* (Phillipsburg, NJ: P&R, 2005) and later volumes.

provide a growing body of resources and modeling for preachers who are catching a passion to preach Christ in all of Scripture. We rejoice that the rich tradition of Christ-centered preaching, to which we hope that this little book will contribute, is far wider than Ed Clowney's circle of influence (even as it is far older[9]).

One Christ, one gospel of grace . . . but many heralds sent out by the King of kings to announce his victory. The preachers who have contributed sermons to this volume are representative of the variety of messengers whom Christ has captured and chiseled to declare God's glory among the nations. Some of us, as you will see, were dragged "kicking and screaming" to the realization that each and every one of the Bible's sixty-six books, given to God's people over a millennium and a half, has a single integrating center, a single Hero, Jesus the Messiah, on whom pivots God's whole agenda to recapture his rebellious realm and re-create his sin-cursed handiwork. Others drank in the Christ-centered character of Scripture just as dehydrated pilgrims in a blazing desert rush to quench their thirst in streams of cool water. Some of us preach in large churches; others in congregations of modest size. Some pastor urban churches; others serve in suburbs or small towns. In some congregations, maturing believers in stable families are in the majority; in some, a significant number of curious but uncommitted non-Christians are present each week. Our congregations are located across the United States: in the Northeast, the Mid-Atlantic, the Midwest, the South, the Southwest, and the West Coast.

The sermons in our collection themselves illustrate the diversity of the Scriptures' witness to Christ. When I contacted these preachers, I asked each to nominate from among his sermons that message that best exemplified the influence of Dr. Clowney on his understanding and proclamation of God's Word. I also asked for the texts of a couple of alternative sermons, in the event that two preachers chose the same Scripture text. Happily, not only was there no such duplication (so every contributor submitted his first choice) but also the passages were distributed nicely across the biblical canon:

9. See Dennis E. Johnson, *Him We Proclaim: Preaching Christ from All the Scriptures* (Phillipsburg, NJ: P&R, 2007), 62–125.

four from the Law of Moses, three from the Prophets,[10] one from the Psalms, two from the Gospels, and one from an Epistle. Discovering the Bible's focus on Jesus and his mission from start to finish illumines both the Scriptures that anticipate his coming and those that testify to his achievement and draw out its implications.

As editor I want to express thanks to several people who have helped bring this project to completion. Thanks first to the Clowney Legacy Corporation board members who envisioned this collection, invited me to serve as editor, suggested names of contributors, and offered helpful advice along the way. (In the fall of 2007, as I sent "When God Promises the Impossible" to my fellow contributors, I also sent it to the members of the board. Not long thereafter I received a hand-written note from Jean Clowney, Ed's widow and a member of the board, expressing appreciation for this first installment of the collection . . . along with a list of insightful editorial corrections that would make the sermon and introduction better! Jean joined Ed in the presence of Christ on June 7, 2008.) Thanks particularly to Helen Holbrook, a member of the Legacy board, for transcribing sermons from audio recordings into text files, greatly facilitating the editing process. Deborah J. Dewart, legal counsel for the Clowney Legacy Corporation board, helped greatly as the Corporation clarified agreements with each preacher who contributed material to this project. As noted in the introduction to the late Dr. Conn's sermon on Isaiah 55, we are grateful to Dr. Conn's daughter, Mrs. Beth Conn Neikirk, for permission to publish his sermon posthumously and for her editorial review of both the sermon and the introduction that I wrote for it. Thanks also to Grace Mullen, assistant librarian and archivist of Westminster Theological Seminary's Montgomery Library, and to the staff of Tenth Presbyterian Church in Philadelphia for providing access to audio-recordings of Dr. Conn's sermons, from which "Thorns and Fir Trees" was selected. Finally, many thanks go to Allan Fisher, senior vice president for

10. When Jesus affirmed to his disciples "that everything written about me in the Law of Moses and the Prophets and the Psalms must be fulfilled" (Luke 24:44, ESV), his reference was to the threefold division of the Hebrew Scriptures (only partially reflected in our English versions, which follow the categories of the Greek Septuagint), in which the Prophets included not only Isaiah, Jeremiah, Ezekiel, and the Minor Prophets, but also the historical narrative books Joshua, Judges, Samuel, and Kings.

book publishing, and the editorial staff of Crossway for venturing to publish this book. As Al has observed, *Heralds of the King* forms a fitting complement to and extension of *Preaching Christ in All of Scripture*, published by Crossway in 2003, since the heart of that work is thirteen of Ed's classic, widely-loved expositions of Christ and the glory of his grace "in all of Scripture." We here join our voices to Dr. Clowney's in extolling the mighty and merciful Redeemer!

Now, listen for the voice of the Good Shepherd, as he calls his sheep by name from the pages of his Word, through heralds whom he has seized by invincible mercy and sent in joy, bearing his message of good news.

A TRIBUTE
TO EDMUND P. CLOWNEY

1917–2005

Theologian, educator, and pastor Edmund P. Clowney was born July 30, 1917, the only child of a Philadelphia cabinetmaker. His academic gifts appeared early, as did his artistic abilities. One of Ed's first jobs was sign-writing for a local grocer. Later he would illustrate Sunday school materials and give evangelistic "Chalk Talks" to seaside crowds.

Ed arrived at Wheaton College certain of his family's Presbyterian faith but unsure of his own role. There, while struggling to meet God's demands, he found a verse in Jonah: "Salvation is of the LORD." That message, of God bestowing life on believers despite their failings, became his central theme. While at Wheaton, Ed met Jean Wright, with whom he would enjoy sixty-three years of marriage. They were to have five children, twenty-one grandchildren, and fifteen great grandchildren.

While Ed gathered degrees not only from Wheaton but also from Westminster Theological Seminary and Yale University Divinity School, and although he later assumed the first presidency of Westminster, he bore himself not as a fusty academic but as a well-humored pastor, approachable and gregarious. His sermons were narrations of a joyous gospel.

Painstaking in his scholarship, Ed's prime concern became to reveal Jesus' presence throughout the Bible (e.g., *Preaching Christ in All of Scripture* and *The Unfolding Mystery*). He wrote ten books and hundreds of articles, many of which have been translated around the world. His last book, *How Christ Transforms the Ten Commandments*, was accepted by the publisher only days before his death.

Ed helped establish satellite seminaries for Westminster in California and Florida, a Reformed seminary in Aix-en-Provence, France, and a theological studies program for urban ministers in a rough section of North Philadelphia. His passion for service led him to relocate four times after his "retirement" in 1984—to teach at Westminster Seminary California, to help at Christ the King Presbyterian Church in Houston, and twice to serve as theologian-in-residence at Trinity Presbyterian Church in Charlottesville, Virginia.

Ed's sense of humor and his love for people was radiant. In the last week of his life, even as speech failed him, he joked with visitors and family by hand signals and wiggled eyebrows. He took much comfort in hymns sung by friends around his bed. Though Ed claimed his high school music teacher once begged him *not* to sing, he was clearly eager to join in that unending doxology his whole life had anticipated.

Ed died March 20, 2005, after a short illness. He was 87.[1]

---

1. Adapted from the Edmund P. Clowney Web site, www.edmundclowney.com/.

CONTRIBUTORS

Arturo G. Azurdia III (D.Min., Westminster Seminary California) is associate professor of pastoral theology and director of pastoral mentoring, Western Seminary, Portland, OR, founder of the seminary's ministry to pastors, The Spurgeon Fellowship, and editor of the *Spurgeon Fellowship Journal* (http://www. thespurgeonfellowship.org/). He previously planted and pastored Christ Community Church in Fairfield, CA. He is the author of *Spirit-Empowered Preaching.*

Harvie M. Conn (Litt.D., Geneva College) (1933–1999) was professor of missions at Westminster Theological Seminary, having previously served as a foreign missionary of the Orthodox Presbyterian Church in South Korea. He authored *Eternal Word and Changing Worlds; Evangelism: Doing Justice and Preaching Grace*; and *Urban Ministry* (coauthor).

Charles D. Drew (M.Div., Westminster Theological Seminary) is pastor of Emmanuel Presbyterian Church in New York, NY, a congregation of the Presbyterian Church in America. He is the author of *The Ancient Love Song: Finding Christ in the Old Testament* and *A Journey Worth Taking: Finding Your Place in This World.*

Iain M. Duguid (Ph.D., Cambridge University) is professor of religion at Grove City College and founding pastor of Christ Presbyterian Church in Grove City, PA, a congregation of the Associate Reformed Presbyterian Church. He is the author of *Living in the Gap between Promise and Reality: The Gospel* *according to Abraham; Living in the Grip of Relentless Grace: The Gospel according to Isaac and Jacob*; and the *Reformed Expository Commentary* volumes on Esther, Ruth, and Daniel.

William Edgar (D.Th., University of Geneva) is professor of apologetics at Westminster Theological Seminary in Philadelphia, PA, and a teaching elder in the Presbyterian Church in America. He is the author of *Truth in All Its Glory: Commending the Reformed Faith; Reasons of the Heart: Recovering Christian Persuasion; The Face of Truth: Lifting the Veil;* and *Les dix commandements.*

Dennis E. Johnson (Ph.D., Fuller Theological Seminary) is professor of practical theology at Westminster Seminary California and an associate pastor of New Life Presbyterian Church in Escondido, CA, a congregation of the Presbyterian Church in America. He is the author of *Him We Proclaim; Triumph of the Lamb;* and *The Message of Acts in the History of Redemption.*

Timothy J. Keller (D.Min., Westminster Theological Seminary) is senior pastor of Redeemer Presbyterian Church in New York, NY, a congregation of the Presbyterian Church in America, having previously taught practical theology at Westminster Theological Seminary. He is the author of *The Reason for God; Ministries of Mercy; Worship by the Book* (coauthor); and *The Prodigal God.*

Julius J. Kim (Ph.D., Trinity Evangelical Divinity School) is associate professor of practical theology, dean of students, and director of the Center for Pastoral Refreshment at Westminster Seminary California, and an associate pastor of New Life Presbyterian Church in Escondido, CA, a congregation of the Presbyterian Church in America. He is a contributor to *Covenant, Justification, and Pastoral Ministry.*

Joseph V. Novenson (M.Div., Westminster Theological Seminary) is senior pastor of Lookout Mountain Presbyterian Church in Lookout Mountain, TN, a congregation of the Presbyterian Church in America.

Joseph F. Ryan (M.Div. and D.D., Westminster Theological Seminary) has pastored Trinity Presbyterian Church in Charlottesville, VA, and Park Cities Presbyterian Church in Dallas, TX. He is a teaching elder in the Presbyterian Church in America, and he has authored *Worship: Beholding the Beauty of the Lord* and *That You May Believe*.

Brian Vos (M.Div., Westminster Seminary California) is pastor of Trinity United Reformed Church in Caledonia, MI, a congregation of the United Reformed Churches in North America. He has contributed articles to periodicals such as *The Outlook, Modern Reformation*, and *Kerux*.

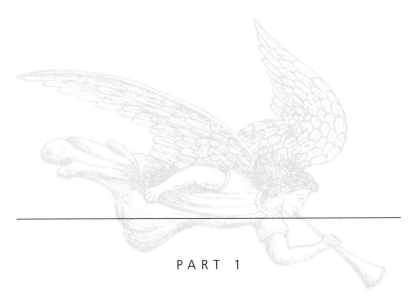

PART 1

THE LAW

1

LIVING WITH A GAP

Genesis 17:1–14

Joseph V. Novenson

Introduction

This message was first preached in Lexington Presbyterian Church in Lexington, SC, as a portion of a Genesis series. It so caught my own heart and mind that I have returned to it to "mine" the riches of the text again and again.

This message has since been delivered in various contexts and edited according to those with whom I would be studying the passage. Believing the issue of living with this gap between our condition and God's calling is an important and oft disregarded reality of Christian living, I have spoken on this topic to Christian educators, to graduates from theological institutions, to parents who are trying to be faithful in their role of discipling children, to student service providers in academic institutions from around the country, and to university students in various contexts. The responses to the sermon have been mixed, but Christians' identification with a gap and its accompanying spiritual and personal ambiguities has been fairly consistent. Believers in Christ seem consciously or unconsciously beleaguered by a growing sense of the enormity of the gap in virtually every context within which we serve. This consistency has served as a bit of a test. I have found this true within both contexts sympathetic to the Reformed tradition and those quite cynical about it. The soul cries out for sovereign grace that the redeemed sinner knows he or she cannot live without, even when the intellect scoffs at its particularities.

I found in Edmund P. Clowney a model of the Christlikeness commanded in Genesis 17 both in his preaching content and in the life he lived, and this made listening to his lectures and sermons stunningly compelling. It was his pleasure in the Old Testament's wonderful disclosing of Christ that I found most compelling. I remember him taking a passage in which I saw little or nothing of my King; and then faithfully he opened it in a way consistent with the text, consistent with the larger story of the narrative, and consistent with all of Scripture—portraying Christ in such a way that I was at times breathless and unable to take notes in class or in worship when he was preaching. I remember going up to him one time after a lecture that had left the realms of academia and entered the glories of preaching. My notes literally degenerated from sentences and concepts connected with the progress of his exegesis, to simply writing, "Glory! Glory! Glory!" When I went up to Dr. Clowney, I simply said, "Please don't give us a test on the lecture today because I couldn't take notes. I was too busy worshiping in light of the Scripture." He simply smiled knowingly as if to say he, too, was equally blessed by the privilege of being taught by the Word of God that he had simply been permitted to expound before us.

I always sensed that Dr. Clowney saw himself as a privileged steward of the mysteries of God. He regularly seemed amazed that he too had been entrusted with the unspeakable glory of preaching, though he never felt worthy in himself to handle the Word of God. He modeled before me this posture: he knew he could not preach the Word without the help of grace through the Spirit's ministry. That overwhelming sense of privileged delight was evident in him and magnetic for me.

I suppose Dr. Clowney's love for the redemptive historic model of preaching is rather well known. But the man himself, whom such a vibrant grasp of truth produced, has perhaps influenced me more than the manner of exegesis and homiletics that he taught. Dr. Clowney was simultaneously one of the most brilliant and gifted men I have ever known, and one of the most thoroughly unimpressed with himself. He was simply swept off his feet by the wonder of his Savior and his salvation, and the meeting of those realities in his life made him a theaterplace for God's glory. I have met few people like him. He walked like his Master because he walked with his Master and talked of his Master with little or no attention to himself. When I was still quite cynical about the particularities of Reformed theology, I remember thinking, *If that man* (meaning Ed Clowney) *is what Reformed theology produces, then I want to understand it.* I listened to others in the Reformed tradition and watched them and got the impression that Reformed theology fostered becoming a "brain on a stick." I listened to still other proponents of Reformed thinking and got the impression that to be "Reformed" was to become a warrior with a weapon, or that it was erudition plus scholarship plus obscurity, wed to formality, which produced eccentricity. In Dr. Edmund P. Clowney, I saw that God's truth more fully understood would make someone more fully like Christ as one more fully understood his Person and work in the wonder of the preached Word of God.

One experience of note has been memorable to me through the years of my privilege of opening the Word of God. I remember standing in front of Dr. Clowney in an early preaching class. When the sermon was over, he gently asked me, "Where was my Savior?" My memory has likely edited the experience significantly. But what followed seemed to be an interminable silence on my part and on the part of the rest of the students in the room. The reality of my having opened the Word of the Savior, designed to disclose the Savior, and having not spoken of the Savior settled on us all. I could only stammer and stutter, and Dr. Clowney very kindly removed the obvious agonizing pressure of conviction that was cutting me to the quick and politely asked to speak with me privately. He then quickly invited the next student to stand and preach, and the moment passed. But when I spoke with him privately, he pressed home the fact that I must never miss any occasion of preaching to proclaim the person of Jesus.

Often now when I enter a pulpit, I quietly ask, "Where is my Savior?"

I will be Ed Clowney's debtor for the first several billion years of eternity for having shown me much of what it means to be a pastor and a preacher who is truly in the Reformed tradition.

The Scripture: Genesis 17:1–14[1]

When Abram was ninety-nine years old, the LORD appeared to him and said, "I am God Almighty; walk before me and be blameless. I will confirm my covenant between me and you and will greatly increase your numbers."

Abram fell facedown, and God said to him, "As for me, this is my covenant with you: You will be the father of many nations. No longer will you be called Abram; your name will be Abraham, for I have made you a father of many nations. I will make you very fruitful; I will make nations of you, and kings will come from you. I will establish my covenant as a everlasting covenant between me and you and your descendants after you for the generations to come, to be your God and the God of your descendants after you. The whole land of Canaan, where you are now an alien, I will give as an everlasting possession to you and your descendants after you; and I will be their God."

Then God said to Abraham, "As for you, you must keep my covenant, you and your descendants after you for the generations to come. This is my covenant with you and your descendants after you, the covenant you are to keep: Every male among you shall be circumcised. You are to undergo circumcision, and it will be the sign of the covenant between me and you. For the generations to come every male among you who is eight days old must be circumcised, including those born in your household or bought with money from a foreigner—those who are not your offspring. Whether born in your household or bought with your money, they must be circumcised. My covenant in your flesh is to be an everlasting covenant. Any uncircumcised male, who has not been circumcised in the flesh, will be cut off from his people; he has broken my covenant."

1. Scripture citations in this sermon are from the NIV.

The Sermon

I was in India during one of the most stirring cross-cultural mission experiences I have ever known. While I was speaking in southern India to the General Conference of the St. Thomas Evangelical Church, the police arrived and vigorously opposed, in their native tongue, my preaching the gospel. Seeing that I was confused due to my linguistic ignorance, an Indian translator calmly explained to me that the police did not want me to continue. Fear immediately shot through me like electricity as I found myself confronted by official opposition to my carrying on ministry. Actually, "terror" seems a reasonable description of my emotional state. With that terror I sensed afresh the enormous gap between my spiritually fragile inner man and the remarkably high calling upon my life as Christ's servant. My fear and his calling seemed separated by an unimaginably huge chasm.

This hardly seemed an appropriate moment to discuss options, but I awkwardly sought counsel from an Indian Christian near me. "What should I do?" I stammered.

He calmly counseled me in great contrast to my obvious abject terror. In a very matter-of-fact manner, he indicated that *his* Bible had a few verses in it that said to keep preaching when people told us to stop. Then, in the same matter-of-fact tone, he inquired whether or not those verses were in *my* Bible as well.

Needless to say, his gentle rebuke to my fear hit me like a brick bat across the bridge of my nose, and I began to cry. I realized, in my fear, that I was now standing where, for thousands of years, my forefathers and foremothers had stood when the authorities ordered them not to preach God's truth. This brief mental connection with Christian history heightened my sense of the gap between my horribly fearful and weak condition and God's incredibly high calling upon my life.

Now it was my turn to stand! Me? No, it couldn't be! It was almost overwhelming. I began a familiar and vigorous internal argument with myself, and all within seconds:

"Who are *you* to preach in a place like this? *You're afraid* to preach when you are told to stop . . . but you just can't give up. . . . Who are *you* to be a representative of Jesus to these brothers and sisters in India?"

"*I can't do this! I need to stop! But I can't! I simply can't!*"

"You bet you can't! What will people think?"

"*Who cares, I don't want to go to jail.*"

"But what about trusting God?"

The gap I was sensing seemed almost to drip from my pores like perspiration. Surely, it was sadly obvious to my Indian brothers and sisters that all I had within me was a frightened, self-absorbed, broken little heart.

Apply my experience to us all because I believe my time in India merely illustrates a foundational and critical question that must be asked by all Christians: how can the living God advance his kingdom through weak and shattered little people like me and like you? Putting it another way: what possible resources does God impart to his church in order that his way and his wonder may advance, despite all the human frailty and failure so obviously present in us, even after we're redeemed?

A vulnerable acknowledgment of one's own sense of the enormity of the gap between our human condition and God's calling raises just such questions. However, it seems, at least to me, that we Christians avoid these questions by committing two errors.

First, we dodge the gap between God's high call and our frailty through false humility. We hide behind what is understood or portrayed as humility when we describe our condition as "far too broken and so terribly weak" and "too foolish or simple" to even enter into any courageous ministry, mercy, sacrifice, or evangelism. Certainly *we* could not serve believers and unbelievers so radically as to change the world. We imply or plainly state our excuse: "I am just too spiritually immature."

Frankly, this has less to do with humility than it does with lack of faith. It may, actually, have its root in unbelief in who God is and what God provides. But this error is so common that it has become accepted and even seen as respectable!

A *second* error of those of us who are already redeemed is a naiveté about sin. The seriousness of one's tragically fallen condition is simply underestimated. When we commit this error as followers of Christ, we actually rely on our own hustle and human effort to live as God's people for long enough and in large enough numbers that we can ignore or demean others' dependence on the power of the Holy Spirit as "unreformed" or "mystical." Such a Christian experience is lived by a kind of teeth-gritting effort for as long as we can keep it up, until eventually we collapse in on ourselves. Functioning for days, weeks, months, or years as if we could possibly accomplish the calling that God has given us without his glorious intrusive grace, we busy ourselves with spiritual activity until the powerless exhaustion from overwork crushes us, our mates, and our families or colleagues. Moral and personal chaos often ensues.

The question looms before us again: how does God advance his kingdom with people as broken as we are, who serve him day in and day out? How does he advance his glorious work through sinners like us, redeemed yet so obviously flawed?

The answer is found in Genesis 17:1–14. There the gap is clearly portrayed, and God's provision for advancing his kingdom is even more gloriously declared. Moses places these two issues in stark contrast.

The Gap Portrayed

To see the gap portrayed, note that Genesis 16 closes with the "father of Israel," "the father of the faithful," Abraham himself, committing an *illegitimate* act built upon *illegitimate* thinking because of the acceptance of *illegitimate* cultural norms that have given rise to an *illegitimate* relationship that produces an *illegitimate* son. And all of this is to actually attempt to "do" *God's* will in accord with *God's* covenant. One might expect Genesis 17 to begin with God saying, "Are you kidding? Who do you think you are? You're fired! You betrayed me."

Instead, the calling of God on Abraham is freshly declared in Genesis 17. It is stunning because it seems that Moses, under the inspiration of the Holy Spirit, intentionally presented God's call to contrast with chapter 16. As one chapter ends with such sad and sinful circumstances, the next begins with a glorious calling. The thirteen year gap between chapters 16 and 17 certainly did not cause

God to forget that Abraham had sought to accomplish the will of God by basically sleeping with the kitchen help, if I may be blunt. Still, God commands him and entrusts him with the responsibility of covenant headship for the people of God. How can this be? How can a holy God use such a twisted servant and call him to such a high and holy task? The answer is found in four things that God provides to advance his kingdom despite the disservice of Abraham.

1. God provides peerless power to advance his cause.
2. God provides peerless transformation to perfect his servants.
3. God gives the always-transforming servant a universal and eternal purpose.
4. God provides a gospel-centered sign to keep the cross and the King vivid in our hearts and minds.

Genesis 17 is arguably the hinge pin of all ministry, for it is quoted ten times in the book of Hebrews, eight times in the book of Galatians, eight times in the book of Romans, and it is a main focus in Peter's sermon at Pentecost. Stephen even brings it up just prior to being stoned to death. Since it is a theological and missiological hinge pin upon which much of redemptive history turns, it should not be surprising that its application is not only for that one moment of time when Abraham walked the earth. It timelessly applies to the advance of God's kingdom itself in and through the lives of all followers of the living God for all time.

Before we examine God's four provisions in Genesis 17, we should note that for Abraham it has been over twenty years since God promised that Abram and Sarai would have a child. The delay itself must have been difficult. Don't we find God's delays enough grounds for our sinful selective disobedience, accompanied by our assumed impunity from guilt? We say, "God, you just are never on time! So I'm going on a little 'vacation' from obedience!" And we do so only because our schedule is different from God's.

Also, Abraham is no longer a young man. He was over 86 years of age as chapter 16 came to a close. Again, don't we rationalize regular extended "vacations" from passionate obedience by assuming, in our spiritual weariness, that our past faithfulness has "earned" our right to coast for a little while, drop our guard, and just barely comply with God's commands? None of this is said to excuse Abraham, but it may cast light on some of the choices that he made. You and I have more in common with him than either he or we would want to admit.

Ask yourself whether the pressures that are upon you have heightened your own awareness of the gap between your human condition and God's calling, and thereby increased your desire to cry out for God's provision. Or, on the contrary, do you increase your accusing of the Lord, implying that your circumstances are really God's own fault and failure? Perhaps you, like me, are never quite so ruthlessly direct with the King about your rationalized sin. Still, search yourself and ask, "What pressures are there to which I yield and then rationalize disobedience and distorted thinking?"

God's Kingdom Plan Revealed

Now let's examine God's provision for advancing his kingdom through people like us, despite our deep corruption.

God Provides Peerless Power to Advance His Cause

Moses introduces the covenant with God's words, "I will confirm my covenant between me and you and will greatly increase your numbers" (Gen. 17:2). Abram then responds in verse 3 by falling face down. God then says to him, "As for me, this is my covenant with you . . ."

God follows that statement with a series of twelve affirmative and definitive statements: "I will, so . . . you will . . ." again and again! There could well be an exclamation point after each declaration of God's promised power.

The sheer repetition is like a rhetorical jackhammer blasting away upon the hardened, self-reliant heart previously shown by Abraham and evident in all humanity. Although God makes the positive statement, "I will, so . . . you will . . . ," twelve times, God could just as well have said it negatively, "You can't, you won't, you shouldn't, and you wouldn't." This is a declaration of sovereignty and a clear affirmation of God's utter power. It also makes me think of a baseball outfielder waving off the teammate soon to collide with him as both reach for the pop fly, repeating a cry in the outfield heard even in the stands; "I got it! I got it! Mine! Mine!" God is saying exactly that to Abraham: "I got it! I got it!" He waves Abraham and you off! Did you hear him? Did you? Or are you still trying to make the catch on your own? Do you feel the chest-heaving exhaustion beginning to cripple your self-centered effort?

Let's apply this more expansively from beyond the text. A quick summary of Scripture reveals that God often discloses the immensity of his peerless power for the sinners whom he has redeemed at the very moment that their corresponding poverty of human ability is most evident. Still, sadly, we choose self reliance and hustle! Yet God seems to time the disclosure of his provided power just in the nick of time.

One example of this paradox may be found as Stephen is about to be stoned in Acts 7. As the soon-to-be martyr nears the moment of unimaginable pain at the hands of unjust treatment, God tears open heaven and gives him a vision of heaven's courtroom with Stephen's Lord rising to his defense, to sustain his faith as he is crushed in utter weakness beneath stones thrown viciously by a crowd gone wild with rage. God tilts Stephen's chin up as if to make him look at the *real and final* courtroom, the *right and accurate* judgment, and the *righteous and truly powerful* Judge rising in his behalf, lest he languish in a foolishly narrow view of life in all its horrible fallenness. God calls Stephen, like Abraham, to behold his peerless power in the midst of human sin.

Similarly, John the Baptist and Peter, James, and John, Jesus' closest disciples, are the only four people in the New Testament to sensibly experience the Trinity. John the Baptist encounters each person of the Trinity at the baptism of Jesus. He sees the Son standing before him and beholds the descending dove, the theophanic appearance of the Holy Spirit, as he hears the Father's voice: "This is my Son, whom I love; with him I am well pleased." Then, on the Mount of Transfiguration, Peter, James, and John likewise experience the Trinity. The Old Testament manifestation of the Holy Spirit, the *shekinah* glory-cloud, the pillar of fire and smoke, encompasses Jesus, the Son, who stands before them. And the Father speaks once again, saying, "This is my Son, whom I love; with him I am well pleased.

Listen to him!" Note that each of these men—John the Baptist, Peter, James, and John—would face their utter weakness and poverty as they were all horribly persecuted for their faith and (with the exception of John the Apostle) eventually martyred.

Think of it! John the Baptist would have his head removed for the maniacal pleasure of Herod. Understandably, John the Baptist would send to Jesus from his prison cell the question, "Are you the one who was to come, or should we expect someone else?" (Luke 7:20). Surely his weakness loomed before him as he sent messengers to put such an inquiry before the Son of God!

James would be the first apostle to lay down his life for Jesus (Acts 12:2). History and legend admittedly combine, but it seems verified that later Peter was horribly martyred under Nero's reign. All three of the apostles closest to Jesus would face the end of their lives in a hurricane force gale of injustice and physical and relational pain. Surely, they looked dead in the eyes at the depths of their human frailty. But the Triune God also reveals himself to them in glory, so each one is given a peerless vision of God in all his Trinitarian power and wonder. I suggest we find here this principle: _God advances his kingdom with weak servants by graciously disclosing his peerless power to sustain, keep, and move them._

To illustrate the principle, think of the protective equipment worn by gymnasts as they practice floor exercises. Athletes must throw the weight of their body in rapid succession, flipping into cartwheels and handsprings and vaults. Without a securely worn protective harness and pulley system held by trained spotters, by which the gymnast can be lifted into the safety of mid-air should he or she fail in the exercise, practicing such events could literally result in serious injury or death. I know because I remember my brief high school participation in gymnastics. After months of practice, I was told by my gymnastics coach, Coach Cunningham, that we all had "graduated from" the safety harness and now would have to begin to practice floor exercise without it. Of course that's the goal for a gymnast. But not me! The next day when gymnastics practice took place, I was definitely absent! I never went back again! You see, I knew that without the harness I would hurt myself, so I never returned. As the saying goes, "My mama didn't raise no dummy!" I didn't want to die! I had to have protective power or my courage to take risks would be gone!

Genesis 17 is God's promise to Abraham that he would *never, ever* remove the harness. God says to his broken servants like Abraham and all of us, "I will . . . I will . . . I will!" How much more spiritual courage, sacrificial risk, committed obedience, profound and vulnerable repentance would mark us if we actually applied such a promise of provision of peerless, kingdom advancing power? I think we'd shock ourselves and the watching world if we were "practicing Calvinists"! We are all "closet Arminians"! People like me, sympathetic to the Reformed position, are so often articulate in *describing* our position; but we fail in our *application* of its implications. My friends in India, of whom I spoke earlier, taught me that God's sovereignty ought to make me look a lot more like Mother Teresa in lifestyle choices. If I believed, really believed, that God never removes his harness, I believe I would be much more "conformed to the likeness of" Jesus himself (Rom. 8:29).

God Provides Peerless Transformation to Perfect His Servants

God transforms his people first in their *person* and then in their *purpose*.

Genesis 17:1, God's covenant disclosure, begins with a command, preceded by a weighty self-identification by God: "I am God Almighty; walk before me[2] and be blameless."[3]

This is a command for peerless transformation. "Blameless" is the English translation in the NIV for *tamim* in Hebrew. Variously translated elsewhere "whole, complete, finished, not missing any essentials," this is a startling command. How can God give such a command to a man who for many previous years has shown himself to be anything but "*tamim*"—anything but blameless, whole, and complete? In fact, Abraham has shown himself to be person-

---

2. *Walk in front of* (like its parallel, "stand in front of") is well chosen. The phrase usually expresses the service or devotion of a faithful servant to his king, be the latter human (1 Kings 1:2; 10:8) or divine (Gen. 5:22, 24; 6:9).

3. *Blameless:* "This Hebrew word, *tāmim*, is used frequently in the sections of the Old Testament dealing with ritual procedure. It is imperative that the animal brought for sacrifice be one that is unblemished." Victor P. Hamilton, *The Book of Genesis: Chapters 1–17*, New International Commentary on the Old Testament (Grand Rapids, MI: Eerdmans, 1990), 461.

ally and repeatedly *missing* faith, integrity, courage, consistency, and obedience.

God shows his answer to this problem in several ways.

First, Abraham has been commanded by one who has just identified himself as "God Almighty." Let's paraphrase God's opening words: "Because I am who I am, all powerful, I command of you to do what you cannot do and to be what you cannot be. For I can and I will give to you that which you do not have so you will be *tamim*. You will be *tamim* because I command it."

This can be likened to Jesus commanding Lazarus to "come forth" from the tomb, though Lazarus had been dead for days. Abraham has spiritual death oozing from almost every choice he's made. His middle name, spiritually speaking, is often "Rigormortis." He is and ever will be *"anti-tamim"*. . . *unless Someone else* has the ability to transform his person, to make him what he cannot be in himself.

This is where the gospel floods him with grace. The apostle Paul addresses this very issue and uses Abraham as his primary illustration when he argues for *imputed righteousness* provided by Almighty God, who is absolutely just and the perfect justifier when he leaves "sins committed beforehand" by people like Abraham "unpunished" and finally punishes Jesus fully for them in the atoning death of Calvary:

> But now a righteousness from God, apart from law, has been made known, to which the Law and the Prophets testify. This righteousness from God comes through faith in Jesus Christ to all who believe. There is no difference, for all have sinned and fall short of the glory of God, and are justified freely by his grace through the redemption that came by Christ Jesus. God presented him as a sacrifice of atonement, through faith in his blood. He did this to demonstrate his justice, because in his forbearance he had left the sins committed beforehand unpunished—he did it to demonstrate his justice at the present time, so as to be just and the one who justifies those who have faith in Jesus.
>
> Where, then, is boasting? It is excluded. On what principle? On that of observing the law? No, but on that of faith. (Rom. 3:21–27)

What then shall we say that Abraham, our forefather, discovered in this matter? If, in fact, Abraham was justified by works, he had something to boast about—but not before God. What does the Scripture say? "Abraham believed God, and it was credited to him as righteousness." (Rom. 4:1–3)

Paul says it explicitly, though not using *tamim*, when he writes that Abraham was "credited" with righteousness—that is, accounted as *tamim*—by God Almighty. Without the gospel, God's command to Abraham is an utter impossibility for a wretch like him—or you, or me. In fact, *any* command without gospel-given grace can never, ever be kept by a sinner, even a redeemed one.

Think about the grand plan of God in Eden. Pre-fall humans were designed to obey in the context and condition of perfect *tamim* with God. We have lost that "completeness" due to sin. But in Christ and in Christ alone, Abraham and you are *given tamim*. Through grace imputed to you once-for-all by the Father and through grace infused by the Spirit, you can and finally do *love* truth and actually start to *want* to sacrifice, and even sense a beginning *growth* toward real honor. We develop yieldedness and surrender to God's kingdom cause, and all because of that imputed righteousness and the infused grace that follows from it. Soon, we find ourselves not merely admiring William Wilberforce, or Amy Carmichael, or John Paton, or Mother Teresa. We yearn with tearful passion to be like them.

I remember Professor John Frame looking me in the eyes at Westminster Seminary in Philadelphia and saying to this young idealistic student, "You want to study Francis Schaeffer. But I want to help make you into another one like him." As God imputes *tamim* to Abraham and us, the Spirit infuses *tamim* into us; and then, as Mr. Frame hoped, we are transformed. Unfortunately, this hope of Mr. Frame's is far from being realized in me, but that's not the point. God can do so if he pleases, and will do so in the end! That *is* the point!

That brings us to the second dimension of *tamim*: God transforms our *purpose*.

Genesis 17:5 reads, "No longer will you be called Abram [great father], your name will be Abraham [father of many nations]. . . ."[4]

---

4. Ibid.: "It is the first time that an individual's name is changed" (464). Hamilton also observes: "We have noted above the shift (v. 1–8) from second singular to second plural . . . most of this section (v. 9–14) is cast in the plural, and the reason for this should be plain. The

Then God speaks of all Abraham's "descendants" and all the "generations" and all those "born in your household or bought with your
money." His purpose is parental and familial, not unlike the purpose
given to Adam in the garden before the fall into sin.

It is also reminiscent of Genesis 15:5, which reads, "He [God]
took him outside and said, 'Look at the heavens and count the
stars—if indeed you can count them. . . . So shall your offspring
be.'" Abraham would now be re-defined by the sort of impact he
would have upon others. Abraham was being told that he would
reassume the responsibility imparted to Adam to be a blessing to
the world by filling it with "God lovers." Hence in Genesis 12:2 God
says, "You will be a blessing."

In essence, Abraham is being told he is no longer a "guest" on
God's planet but joins God's great mission to advance his kingdom,
and hence becomes a "host." Abraham, like Jesus himself, is not here
to be served but to serve and to give his life for many. God is utterly
redefining the Middle Eastern bedouin named Abram to make him
a servant for the accomplishment of God's kingdom purposes. His
name will be "Abraham." Five times he is told to be and to see himself as the *father* of many nations."

One might conclude that the name change of Abram to "father
of *many* nations" is a purely metaphoric adjustment of title and
has no reference to any God-intended methodological approach to
ministry that would be clearly familial, loving, and warm. But that
position disregards the weight of redemptive history, which, when
read as context for this name change, seems clearly to teach a rich,
warm, and robust familial approach to all ministry associated with
Abraham's descendants. So let's first examine a redemptive historic
sketch of the familial fabric of God's kingdom advancement. Then,
we'll apply its implications.

Redemptive Historic Summary on the Familial Character
of God's Kingdom Program

Even *before creation* the Triune God, who would create image
bearers called humans, already had an "eternal familial quality" as

---

prescriptions covered in these verses are to become legally incumbent upon all generations.
God is speaking to those who are not yet born" (468).

the Father, *the* Son, and *the* Holy Spirit, as he would later reveal himself in the Bible. Familial relating, communicating, and loving within the Trinity precede creation, and in fact cause creation. If, then, God ever takes his name "father" and gives it to someone else, how important might you reckon *that* to be?

At creation Genesis begins with a family, Adam and Eve, commanding them to *love*, in order to fill the earth with God lovers as the Triune God's image bearers. They will be physically "one" as their God is mysteriously and perfectly one, and children born from their union will love God and fill the earth . . . if sin and death have not intervened.

As history progresses the repeated genealogies of the Torah show the importance of family structure, naming in detail a host of otherwise unknown individuals. Noah is given the same familial command previously given to Adam and Eve. Now Noah hears it post-flood. He is to repopulate the world with God lovers in a familial way.

Within our study of Genesis 17, Abraham's name is indicative of a familial fabric of this new kingdom, for he is not named "*leader* of many nations" or "*pastor* of many nations." He is not called "*prophet, priest,* or *king* of many nations," as important as these titles are. Abraham's title is not ecclesiastical, civil, governmental, or professional. It is clearly familial.

The covenants God makes with his people progress through family ties from Abraham, to Isaac, then on to Jacob and his sons, and to the tribes and clans that they father. Joseph rescues his brothers in familial faithfulness and affection, despite their bizarre familial trespass against him. Moses is commanded to arrange the tent city of nomadic Israel in the wilderness by tribes, which are merely big families. Joshua enters the land and divides it up familially according to tribes. The family theme continues in the Psalms and the Prophets:

> *Psalm 68:4–6* reads: "His name is the LORD. . . . A father to the fatherless, a defender of widows. . . . God sets the lonely in families. . . ." *Isaiah 66:13* records God's poignant reassurance to errant Israel: "As a mother comforts her child, so will I comfort you. . . ."

Hosea the prophet points us to God's familial way of redeeming a people at great personal loss, even when the one whom Hosea loves is reprehensible, like the Lord's wandering wife, Israel.

In the New Testament Jesus is revealed to us as our "older brother" and the "first born among many brothers," who is not ashamed to call us "brothers" and who makes us "co-heirs with him" by "adoption" into a "new family." He will conclude his redemptive restorative work with a familial "wedding feast" to which we are invited and for which we are being prepared as a "bride." James records in his epistle that true religion is "to look after widows and orphans in their distress and to keep oneself from being polluted by the world" (James 1:27). True religion has a familial focus to restore broken families. Officers in the New Testament church are required not so much to pass certain seminary courses, but rather to love and care for their families (1 Timothy 3; Titus 1).

Jesus prays that the Trinitarian familial love among the persons of the Godhead, specifically between the Father and the Son, would be experientially normative among us, so we are to be as Jesus prayed: "one, Father, as you are in me and I am in you. . . . May they be brought to complete unity to let the world know that you sent me and have loved them even as you have loved me" (John 17:21–23). Jesus wants the love the Father has for the Son to be in us (v. 26).

Paul says it perhaps most directly as he connects God's familial care to ours in Ephesians 5:1–2: "Be imitators of God, therefore, as dearly loved children and live a life of love, just as Christ loved us and gave himself up for us. . . ."

Now, let's apply. The sheer weight of redemptive historic momentum shown in this brief summary casts light on Abraham's new name by giving context from a much larger picture. We simply must conclude that God is saying, "My kingdom will advance with familial treatment of people within and even outside the covenant community." Cold, sterile, professional, antiseptic, task focused, relationally distant, personally unconcerned ministry practice is inherently forbidden and contradicts the very personality of the Triune God!

This kingdom is to pulse with familial affection, sacrifice, and relational involvement that should find no human cultural peer at any point in history, or in any place on planet Earth. There is to be only one community where creatures can love like the Creator: the kingdom of God.

Unreconciled, bitter, or faction-filled believers do nothing less than lie about the King and his kingdom before they've said a word! More pointedly, our relational dissonance or distance *models heresy*, though our words may be utterly orthodox.

Dr. Cornelius Van Til once stated in a lecture I attended at Westminster Theological Seminary in Philadelphia, "All truth is the externalization of the personality of the Trinity." I was so struck by those words that I could not take notes for the remainder of the class. His brilliant presuppositional statement is reflected in the renaming of Abraham. God, *who is the Father*, is renaming *a father* to carry out his kingdom *family* agenda in a *familial* way because every family reflects the parent. This "family" has no less than God himself as our Father. Glory be to God on high! How dare we act in contradiction to his character and think it acceptable?

Time and time again this familial approach for world transformation is magnified in the Word of God. This is exemplified by the apostle Paul in Romans 9:3 as he calls the unbelieving race of Israel, to which he is seeking to proclaim the gospel, his "brothers." Paul says, "I wish that I myself were cut off from Christ for the sake of *my brothers*, those of my own race." The apostle does not use this word "brothers" loosely. He appears to be adopting the familial approach to world transformation delineated in the Abrahamic covenant and applying it even to some people who want to kill him. Simply put, Paul is implying with this language that, if there is not a deep and abiding love for those served in mission, then we are not doing ministry in accord with the prescription laid out before Abraham by the living God in Genesis 17.

The apostle Paul again exemplifies this kind of familial care for his flock when he describes himself in 1 Thessalonians 2:7–8: "We were gentle among you, like a mother caring for her little children. We loved you so much that we were delighted to share with you not only the gospel of God but our lives as well, because you had become so dear to us." He is even more pointedly familial in verse 17, when he writes about the separation from Thessalonica as follows: "But, brothers, when we were *torn away* from you for a short time (in person, not in thought), out of our intense longing we made every effort to see you." The words "torn away" are a translation of one word, *aporphanizō*. At its heart is the Greek word *orphan*, which is the source of our English word for a child who has lost parents. It calls to mind the media pictures of parents being separated from a child by some unjust court order requiring that the child be wrenched from his loving parents' hands while they reach yearningly for the child, screaming over the separation. This is the picture Paul paints of leaving the Thessalonian church. So God advances his kingdom with people who have been designed to address the world with a familial-like love that has no peer.

Puritan history exemplifies this familial approach to ministry. In the 1780 collection of the letters from John Newton originally entitled *Voice of the Heart: Cardiphonia*, there is a biographical sketch in which the Rev. R. Cecil frankly assesses Newton's weaknesses as a preacher:

> With respect to his ministry, he appeared, perhaps, to least advantage in the pulpit, as he did not generally aim at accuracy in the composition of his sermons, nor at any address in the delivery of them. His utterance was far from clear, and his attitude ungraceful.[5]

Newton's biographer is quick to add, however:

> He possessed, however, so much affection for his people, and zeal for their best interests, that the defect of his manner was of little consideration with his constant hearers. At the same time, his capacity, and habit of entering into their trials and experience, gave the highest interest to his ministry among them. . . . The *parent-like tenderness and affection* which accompanied his instruction made them prefer him to preachers who, on other accounts, were much more generally popular. . . . His ministerial visits were exemplary. I do not recollect one, though favored with many, in which his general infor-

---

5. R. Cecil, "Memoirs of the Rev. John Newton," in *The Works of the Rev. John Newton to Which Are Prefixed Memoirs of His Life by the Rev. R. Cecil, A.M.* (Thomas Nelson & Peter Brown: Edinburgh, 1827), 68. Also cited in John Newton, *Voice of the Heart: Cardiphonia* (repr., Chicago: Moody, 1950), 18. Previous editions published under the title *Cardiphonia*, various publishers.

mation and lively genius did not communicate instruction, and his
affectionate and condescending sympathy did not leave comfort.[6]

In other words, John Newton ministered in a familial way to his
flock. John Newton himself commented on his manner of gently
and lovingly ministering to people even from the pulpit, relative
to his peers: "Perhaps it is better to feed our people like chickens,
a little and often, than to cram them like turkeys, till they cannot
hold one gobbet more."[7]

How this approach might well temper our pulpits and blogs and
lectures as we expound and apply the Word of God in the Father's
church! The familial purpose should be evident in all we do!

O Jesus, forgive our antiseptic professionalism and scholastic
sterility!

God Gives the Always-Transforming Servant a Universal and Eternal Purpose

Abraham is not only redefined by his impact on others and commanded to do so in a familial way; he is to do so without accepting
any cultural, racial, linguistic, or social barrier whatsoever. The impact
that God's kingdom advance is to have upon the world is universal.
It is in the DNA of God's kingdom people to be *omnicultural*.

In Genesis 17:4, we read that Abraham is to be "the father of
many nations." This is repeated in verse 6, where he is told, "I will
make *nations of you*." Hence, he is to be ministering in a multicultural
manner, to say the very least. But in Genesis 12:3 God told Abraham,
"*all* peoples on earth will be blessed through you." We see Abraham's
calling as not only multicultural, but it is *omnicultural*. For Abraham
to live in a parochial, self-absorbed, monocultural manner would
betray the transforming work of God's advancing kingdom. Every
human and sin-made barrier must fall before God's advancing kingdom. Babel's dispersal will be undone by God's grand reversal.

This means that the late missiology professor of Westminster
Seminary, Dr. Harvey Conn, was right when he said, "The kingdom
of God is not uniform, but unified." Cults are uniform, but the

6. Cecil, "Memoirs," 68 (emphasis added).
7. Newton, *Voice of the Heart*, 21.

kingdom is unified. This multinational view is so prominent, that when God speaks in Genesis 25:23 about the children inside of the beloved Rebekah's womb, he does not say there are two children within her. He says, "Two *nations* are in your womb."

This omnicultural ministry, empowered by God, is also *eternal*. Genesis 17:7 calls this promise of such empowering grace from God to love and serve every nation "an *everlasting* covenant." Verse 8 promises "everlasting" placement on the earth. Verse 13 identifies the sign of this promise as "everlasting." There is therefore, no "plan B," no exceptions, no options or alternatives . . . now or ever.

What a privilege! What an honor it is to be placed into the longest standing, most multilingual, multinational, multiracial, multicultural organization in the history of the cosmos, the kingdom of God! This kingdom will be among God's tools to heal the cosmos, and you and I are placed in it! This alone should thrill us and motivate us by glorious privilege to passionate obedience and service.

This provision of God means that the slightest hint of racism is hereby condemned as abject heresy among God's people. Mono-cultural or single race supremacy of any kind is an aberration. Cul-tural elitism is a contradiction of our kingdom calling, both then and now, because God's people are to participate in a kingdom that is universal, and this intent of God is eternal.

When God's people have been gripped by this thrust of God's advancing kingdom, they have often been lonely voices among the overt and covert cultural racists of their moment in history. In the 1800s the Scottish Presbyterian missionary, John G. Paton, exem-plified this commitment to God's omnicultural kingdom, standing all but alone amidst the culturally self-impressed of his age. As he both went to and returned from the ministry to the New Hebrides and their cannibalistic cultures, he received mixed response and even rejection among his own race and denomination for his care for "brutes." When he traveled to Australia for prayer support and fund-raising, he found church members who doubted that aborigi-nal tribes' people even had souls. Thankfully, in a visit to England he would find a Baptist brother and sister named Reverend and Mrs.

Charles H. Spurgeon, who would support him when some closer to him in theological persuasion would not![8]

Reverend Paton wrote:

> A book once fell into my hands, entitled, "Sermons on Public Subjects," by Charles Kingsley. I knew him to be a man greatly gifted and greatly beloved; and hence my positive distress on reading from the eighth sermon, page 234, "On the Fall," the following awful words: "The Black People of Australia, exactly the same race as the African Negro, cannot take in the Gospel. . . . All attempts to bring them to a knowledge of the true God have as yet failed utterly. . . . Poor brutes in human shape . . . they must perish off the face of the earth like brute beasts." I will not blame this great preacher for boldly uttering and publishing what multitudes of others show by their conduct that they believe, but dare not say so.[9]

Paton ministered in utter contrast to these prejudices in such passion and in such deep commitment to the universal nature of God's kingdom advancement that when he left Australia he could write:

> At my farewell meeting in Melbourne, Sir Henry Barkley presiding, I pleaded that the Colony should put forth greater efforts to give the Gospel to the Aborigines: I showed the idols which I had discovered amongst them; I read Nora's letters; and I may, without presumptions, say, the "brute-in-human-shape" theory has been pretty effectually buried ever since.[10]

May Paton's confidence be found true of us. Would that we were changed by the Abrahamic covenant and never saw another human as a "brute-in-human-shape"!

Social statisticians estimate that the North American Anglo citizens will be the racial minority within twenty to fifty years, conservatively speaking. God is bringing the nations to North America. The sovereign placement of God's people in an omnicultural kingdom ought to thrill us with the prospect of our cities, our neighborhoods,

---

8. John G. Paton, *Missionary Patriarch: The True Story of John G. Paton, Evangelist for Jesus Christ to the South Sea Cannibals* (1891; repr. Vision Forum: San Antonio, 2002), 434–35.

9. Ibid., 263–64.

10. Ibid., 275.

and our churches going through cultural shifts. As Christians, we should be the first at the door to welcome our neighbors who look, dress, speak, and act so differently from us. We should be the first to flex, serve, respect, welcome, and "love our neighbors as ourselves," like a family.

However, with all that God has provided, outlined thus far in Genesis 17, we often fail miserably. We live frightened, self-absorbed, culturally sequestered little (*very* little) lives. We do not live "large," which seems to be the call of the Abrahamic covenant!

"God, I'm a failure! God, we are failures! Help me!"

He does! He does! He does help us!

God Provides a Gospel-Centered Sign to Keep the Cross and the King Vivid in Our Hearts and Minds

As a groom places a "sign of covenant" and love on his bride's finger, so God gives a gospel-driven, christocentric sign to remind his bride that he will pay the price necessary for all of her failings, her sins, her false starts and inexcusable stops. Hence he commands circumcision as the sign of the covenant. The text reads in Genesis 17:9, "As for you, you must keep my covenant. . . ."[11] Then verses 10 and 11, "This is my covenant with you and your descendants after you, the covenant you are to keep: Every male among you shall be circumcised. You are to undergo circumcision, and it will be the sign of the covenant between me and you."

How stunning this is when you see it in context! After twelve "I will . . . you will" statements, God's *primary requirement* of Abraham is to bear the sign of *God's faithfulness* to the covenant, not Abraham's faithfulness. His role is to point himself and his family and everyone in the kingdom to the covenant faithfulness of God. His role is to bear the sign that points away from *his* ability and toward *God's* ability to deal somehow with our sin. Abraham knew of this dealing with sin in such a limited way, through the foreshadowing that he glimpsed in the sign of circumcision. You and I, however,

---

11. Hamilton, *Genesis*, 468, comments on verse 9: "*For your part.* The emphatic pronoun *'attâ* puts the spotlight on Abraham. After a series of "I will's" by God, Abraham becomes the subject of the verb, instead of an object."

know of this so much better, for we know the truths of salvation to which the sign points.

But for now, note that this sign places Abraham in a position much like the transportation department worker who stands on a road under repair, holding a sign that points *away* from the workers as they wave drivers off, a sign that points *to* where drivers should direct their attention. Abraham similarly is to direct attention *away* from humans *to* God's faithfulness. What's the direction of your life's signage? Do you attract people's attention to you or to Jesus? Do you take center stage in your ministry, or do you gladly step aside as God's power is seen elsewhere: in other people, in other elders, in other staff? Your ministry and life point somewhere! Dare to ask yourself, "To whom does my life point?"

The sign itself is shocking![12] I think we must admit it. Though culturally common then, still circumcision is stunning. I suspect that I might have responded to God by saying, "What! Did you say that the sign of the covenant is circumcision? Excuse me, but that seems a bit strange. Perhaps I can understand that you want to remind me that there will be no forgiveness for my sins without the shedding of blood, but please prick my *finger* or my *ear lobe* or perhaps my *heel*. Why such a sign? Why *there*? This is a bit odd!"

No, on the contrary: rather than odd, it is supremely brilliant and pointedly vivid!

To explain this, we must refer to Colossians 2:11 and the following verses that identify the *cross of Jesus Christ* as "a circumcision [not] done by the hands of men." So, connect the dots! We infer that God is saying in Genesis 17 by this sign that no God-ordered ministry will be done, or can be done, without remembering the cross. He seems to be telling us:

1. We must remember the cross so vividly . . . it is even scarred into the flesh. The law was merely nailed to doorposts or woven into hair and head garments.[13] But the gospel is "cut" deeply into our person.

12. Ibid., 470–71.
13. Ibid., 473–74.

2. We must remember the cross in a place (the location of the sign) in which we will not often think of spirituality and theology and truth and God.

3. During our moments of sexual intimacy with our spouse, we should even be mindful of the cross.

4. We must remember the cross at the moment a child is conceived.

5. We must remember the cross every time we change a diaper.

6. We must be "cross-eyed" as we look at all children and every marriage and experience of human love and physical intimacy and passionate sexuality and family.

7. Basically, we should only be able to look at *all of life* "cross-eyed."

I have personally evaluated my grasp of God's intent with this sign by asking all three of my children, who are now grown, to leave the room on one evening during family devotions when they were quite young. I invited them back into the room one at a time so none of them could hear their siblings as I asked them a single question; "What is the most important truth that I have taught you as your father?" My eldest son said to me, "Always do the right thing!" My younger son said, "Always keep the rules and do your best." But my youngest child, my daughter, then in preschool, simply said, "Jesus loves me." I looked at my wife and said in sorrow, "Great! I've raised two Pharisees and one Christian." Although in many ways that is an oversimplification, there is great truth in it. It is an oversimplification because all three of my children have become believers in Jesus Christ. Thanks be to the Sovereign King of grace and glory!

But the truth of this statement is measured by this: The emphasis in raising my first two children was far more upon our rule-keeping than upon the Savior reigning. It was far more upon obedience than it was upon delight in a sovereign, electing salvation. It was far more upon externals than it was upon internals. It was far more upon acting so that I would respond to them favorably than on their believing so that faith would immensely deepen them in obedience. It took me three children before I became more faithful to God's covenant and its sign in the way that I saw family and marriage and parenting. How about you, Dad or Mom? Are you "cross-eyed"?

Failures like us are called and commissioned because the cross is sufficient. Remember! Remember! That's the reason for this sign. God will advance his kingdom as the gospel is made clear for the forgiveness of sins to the sinner and the magnification of Christ's work is made vivid to the broken. We are to constantly think of the perfection of saints by imputed righteousness, or we'll give up. Even in physical places where most folks don't consider Christ at all. We must remember the gospel! Then the self-reliant human heart will beat out a rhythm that stops being utterly contradictory to sovereign, electing grace. That's what circumcision was to teach. If we as failed servants are covered by grace, we should be the biggest, fastest, deepest repenters the world has ever seen.

Conclusion

There is peerless privilege to be savored by us who have been so graciously rescued, when these ways of God's advancing his kingdom are graciously given us. It is much like purchasing tickets for your very favorite musical performance with a favorite artist. Perhaps it is a classic, Celtic, folk, jazz, or bluegrass concert. No matter. You have invested a significant amount of money, and you're still only in the "nosebleed seats" in the third balcony. Imagine, for the sake of illustration, in the midst of the concert, the performer you so enjoy and have finally come to see in person addresses the audience just before the intermission with the following words: "Is the following person here?" and then the artist says *your name*. Just imagine the shock and even terror that might course through your heart and mind, having heard your name coming from his or her lips in that massive auditorium. This would probably be paralyzing. But then imagine that the performer whom you so deeply love and profoundly respect says the following: "I know you're here. I know you bought a ticket. I made sure you got that ticket." A spotlight begins to sweep through the entire audience until it finally locates you sitting in the balcony. Your sense of embarrassment is now almost intolerable, and then the performer who has captured your heart and imagination for so many years affectionately says these words to you: "There you are. I am so glad I found you. I would like to invite you to come down onto the stage to play and sing this next song with me!" Can you even imagine the swirling sense of terror, privilege, and joy that would course through you?

May I tell you something even more marvelous that has happened? The living God has turned to you, Christian, weak and broken sinner that you are, and called upon you to sing the music of the gospel before the entire world. His electing grace has sovereignly found you and made you his own; and he has now commanded you to sing a "life music" that is familial and universal, unstopped by racial or social barriers, a melody that is driven by a gospel attention that is life-constraining. He wants you to play his song before the world. Do you sense the privilege? You see, you and I will never play the music of his kingdom any better than a middle school band member plays Beethoven's *Fifth Symphony*. Have you ever listened to middle-schoolers play Beethoven? Someone has said wisely, "It's music only a father could love."

The miracle is, the Father *does* love the music that you sing, and he will actually change the world when people hear you singing the song. He will make sure they hear his message in your song. Welcome to the "band," fellow follower of the Most High God! Take your place in his orchestra with a fresh sense of his full provision, and play with pleasure!

2

THE GIRL NOBODY WANTED

Genesis 29:15–35

Timothy J. Keller

Introduction

I first preached on this text in the late 1970s in my fledgling pastoral charge in Hopewell, Virginia. The congregation held the traditional three preaching services every week—Sunday morning, Sunday evening, and Wednesday evening, and each weekly service required a fresh Bible exposition. Looking back on this, I now see what an invaluable discipline this was. In the nine years I was there (1974–1984), I preached through most of the Bible. Wednesday nights were usually dedicated to covering the Old Testament, and that is where I was forced to grapple with Ed Clowney's challenge to "preach Christ" from all of Scripture.

I had met Ed when I was a new believer involved in InterVarsity Christian Fellowship at Bucknell University in central Pennsylvania.

In 1970 there had been a small revival on campus, and the Inter-Varsity group had gone from about twelve to fifteen attenders to nearly one hundred in just a few months. We decided to do a major evangelistic outreach and chose as our theme "The Christian and the Absurd Man." Existentialism à la Camus and Sartre was very "hot" on campus, and we wanted to find a Christian speaker who could show familiarity with its perspective and give a Christian response to it.

Some members of our fellowship had heard of Ed Clowney, president of Westminster Seminary in Philadelphia, just three hours or so away by car. I corresponded with him, and he agreed to come and give the lecture. The room where the lecture was held was packed out with 150 people—standing room only. Ed was shocked at the size ("I am used to about ten students for these events," he told me), but proceeded to deliver one of the best talks I had ever heard. He showed intimate knowledge of existentialist writings, but boldly said that "absurd existence" was not so much our noble lot as our curse. When the talk was over, we invited non-Christians present to come to a weekend retreat in which Ed would speak on the nature of the gospel. About twenty came, and the discussions and interactions were rich. One girl gave her life to Christ on the retreat after speaking long and earnestly with a patient, listening Ed.

Ed was delighted with the whole experience and told me he had never been involved with such a well-conceived and successful student mission. When I told him I was thinking of ministry and seminary, he did not push Westminster on me. When he discovered I wasn't Reformed and wasn't thinking of the Presbyterian ministry, he told me of several good seminaries besides Westminster. I eventually chose Gordon-Conwell and began there in 1972. In the summer of 1973 I ran into him speaking at a conference at Pinebrook, in the Pennsylvania Poconos. I approached him sheepishly (having gone to another seminary), but he took me aside for a soda and showed great interest in me and my training and spiritual development. I was deeply touched.

The following year he came to Gordon-Conwell and delivered the Staley lectures on Preaching Christ from the Old Testament. My future wife Kathy (then a student with me) and I were blown away by his teaching. We received from him one of the three or four main ingredients for our own future ministry. I had taken several courses with Richard Lovelace that had revealed the difference between moralistic religiosity (even of a doctrinally sound, biblical sort) and gospel-renewal. Now, in Clowney, I realized I had discovered the application of this distinction to preaching. Moralistic sermons worked only on the will, but Christ-centered preaching clarified the gospel and changed the heart.

However, as most disciples of Ed Clowney have learned, the execution of his vision is extremely hard! How do you "get to Christ" in a way that truly honors the authorial intent in the particular text, without allegorizing or just simply "tacking Jesus on" at the end? It was in these nine years of Old Testament expositions that I struggled with the difficulty of "preaching Christ" from the text, not only with integrity, but also with practicality. Even when you could figure out how Christ was the fulfillment of the theme of the text, how do you get to application? Many Christ-centered sermons are hermeneutically sound and uplifting but leave you without knowing what difference it will all make to how you live your life on Monday.

By the time I came to New York City to plant Redeemer Presbyterian Church, I had worked through these questions and come to my own ways of answering them. One of the sermons that made me feel I was finally being true to Clowney's vision was the following sermon on Jacob's unloved wife, Leah, "The Girl Nobody Wanted." I originally preached it on a unique occasion. Redeemer's first staff member, Yvonne Dodd, married Rick Sawyer in the middle of a Sunday morning service. I was faced with a problem. There have always been lots of single people in my church who want to be married but haven't been able to find a spouse. Many of them struggle desperately with this. How could I do a wedding in the worship service without rubbing their noses in their own unwanted singleness? I wanted to do a sermon that spoke to the limits of what marriage can bring, about our true Spouse in heaven and his love. I chose this sermon because I had recently preached through Genesis in a series of lunch-time weekday meetings and had hit upon a way to understand Leah as not only someone *pointing* us to Christ (as the rejected one through whom salvation came into the world) but also as someone *looking* to the Lord as her true Spouse.

For three years in the late '90s, Ed Clowney and I taught a week-long D.Min. course on preaching at Reformed Seminary in Orlando, Florida. One day, with Ed listening, I preached "The Girl Nobody Wanted" to the class as a sermon case-study. Afterwards he said to me that, while he had never thought through that text, if he had, he would have preached it along those lines. After all those years of struggling to preach in this way, it was one of the most comforting and encouraging statements I have ever received from anyone in my life.

The Scripture (Genesis 29:15–35)[1]

Laban said to him, "Just because you are a relative of mine, should you work for me for nothing? Tell me what your wages should be."

Now Laban had two daughters; the name of the older was Leah, and the name of the younger was Rachel. Leah had weak eyes, but Rachel was lovely in form, and beautiful. Jacob was in love with Rachel and said, "I'll work for you seven years in return for your younger daughter Rachel."

Laban said, "It's better that I give her to you than to some other man. Stay here with me." So Jacob served seven years to get Rachel, but they seemed like only a few days to him because of his love for her.

Then Jacob said to Laban, "Give me my wife. My time is completed, and I want to lie with her."

So Laban brought together all the people of the place and gave a feast. But when evening came, he took his daughter Leah and gave her to Jacob, and Jacob lay with her. And Laban gave his servant girl Zilpah to his daughter as her maidservant.

When morning came, there was Leah! So Jacob said to Laban, "What is this you have done to me? I served you for Rachel, didn't I? Why have you deceived me?"

Laban replied, "It is not our custom here to give the younger daughter in marriage before the older one. Finish this daughter's bridal week; then we will give you the younger one also, in return for another seven years of work."

And Jacob did so. He finished the week with Leah, and then Laban gave him his daughter Rachel to be his wife. Laban gave his

---

1. Scripture citations in this sermon are from the NIV.

servant girl Bilhah to his daughter Rachel as her maidservant. Jacob lay with Rachel also, and he loved Rachel more than Leah. And he worked for Laban another seven years.

When the LORD saw that Leah was not loved, he opened her womb, but Rachel was barren. Leah became pregnant and gave birth to a son. She named him Reuben, for she said, "It is because the LORD has seen my misery. Surely my husband will love me now."

She conceived again, and when she gave birth to a son she said, "Because the LORD heard that I am not loved, he gave me this one too." So she named him Simeon.

Again she conceived, and when she gave birth to a son she said, "Now at last my husband will become attached to me, because I have borne him three sons." So he was named Levi.

She conceived again, and when she gave birth to a son she said, "This time I will praise the LORD." So she named him Judah. Then she stopped having children.

The Sermon

There is no book, I believe, less sentimental about marriage and the family than the Bible. It is utterly realistic about how hard it is not to be married; and it is utterly realistic about how hard it is to be married. Out in the world, especially in the culture outside of the church, there are a lot of people who are cynical about marriage. They don't trust marriage, so they avoid it altogether or give themselves an easy escape by living together. Then there are people inside the church who are very much the opposite. They think, "Marriage, family, white picket fences—that is what family values are all about. That's how you find fulfillment. That is what human life is all about."

The Bible says that both of those attitudes are wrong. It does not hold up marriage and the family as what you need to have a fulfilled life. The Bible shows us marriage and the family, with all of its joys and all of its difficulties, and points us to Jesus and says, "This is who you need, this is what you need, to have a fulfilled life." What the Bible says is so nuanced, so different, so off the spectrum. One of the places you see that is in this fascinating story—the account of Jacob's search for his one true love. I would like you to notice three things in the story: first, this overpowering human drive to find one true love; secondly, the devastation and disillusionment that ordinarily accompanies the search for true love; and finally, what we can do about this longing.

The Human Drive to Find One True Love

At the beginning of the passage, Laban says to Jacob, "Just because you are a relative of mine, should you work for me for nothing? Tell me what your wages should be" (v. 15). Before continuing, let me give you the backstory. Two generations earlier, God had come to Abraham, Jacob's grandfather, and said, "Abraham, look at the world. Look at the misery, the death, and the brokenness. I am going to do something about it. I am going to redeem this world, and I am going to do it through *your* family, through one of your descendents. And therefore, in every generation of your descendents, *one* child will bear the Messianic line. That child will walk before me and be the head of the clan and pass the true faith on to the next generation. Then there will be another child that bears the Messianic line and another, until one day, one of your descendents will be *the* Messiah himself, *the* King of kings."

Abraham fathered Isaac, the first in the line of Messianic forebears, and when Isaac's wife, Rebekah, became pregnant with twins, God spoke to Rebekah through a prophecy and said, "The elder will serve the younger." That was God's way of saying that the second twin born would be the chosen one, to carry on the Messianic hope. Esau is born first and then Jacob, but in spite of the prophecy, Isaac set his heart on the oldest son. He set his heart on Esau and favored him all through his life. As a result, he distorted his entire family. Esau grew up proud, spoiled, willful, and impulsive; Jacob grew up rejected and resentful and turned into a schemer; Rebekah favored her younger son and became alienated from her husband Isaac.

Finally, the time came for the aged Isaac to give the blessing to the head of the clan, which was to be Esau; but Jacob dressed up as Esau, went in, and got the blessing. When Esau found out about it, he became determined to kill Jacob, and Jacob had to flee into the wilderness. Now everything was ruined. Jacob's life was ruined. Not only did he no longer have a family to be the head of; he no longer had a family or an inheritance at all, and he had to flee for his life.

Jacob did not know whether Esau messed up or he messed up or Isaac or maybe even God, but now his life was in ruins and he would never fulfill his destiny. Just to survive, he was forced to flee to the other side of the Fertile Crescent.

Jacob escaped to his mother's family, and they took him in as a kind of charity case. Laban, his uncle, allowed him to be a shepherd. Laban realized that Jacob had tremendous ability as a shepherd and a manager. He figured out that he could make a lot of money if Jacob were in charge of his flocks. That is how we get to this question: "How much can I pay you to be in charge of my flocks?"

Jacob's answer is basically one word: *Rachel.* He wanted Rachel as his bride, and he was willing to work seven years for her. What do we know about Rachel? The text comes right out and says that Rachel was lovely in form and beautiful. The Hebrew word translated "form" is quite literal; it means exactly what you think. It is talking about her figure. Rachel had a great figure. She had a beautiful face and was absolutely gorgeous. I want to give credit where credit is due and say that Robert Alter, the great Hebrew literature scholar at Berkeley, has helped me understand this text a lot.[2] Alter says there are all sorts of signals in the text about how over-the-top, intensely lovesick and overwhelmed Jacob is with Rachel. There is the poignant but telling statement where the text says, "Jacob served seven years to get Rachel, but they seemed like only a few days to him because of his love for her" (v. 20). More interesting is the next verse: "Then Jacob said to Laban, 'Give me my wife. My time is completed, and I want to lie with her.'" Of course that means he wants to have sex with her. Alter says that this statement is so bald, so graphic, so sexual, so over-the-top and inappropriate and non-customary that, over the centuries, Jewish commentators have had to do all kinds of backpedaling to explain it. But he says it is not that hard to explain the meaning. He says that the narrator is showing us a man driven by and overwhelmed with emotional and sexual longing for one woman.

What is going on here? Jacob's life was empty. He never had his father's love. Now he didn't even have his mother's love, and he

---

2. Robert Alter, *Genesis: Translation and Commentary* (New York: W. W. Norton, 1996), 151–57.

certainly had no sense of God's love. He had lost everything—no family, no inheritance, no nothing. And then he saw Rachel, the most beautiful woman he had ever seen, the most beautiful woman for miles around, and he said to himself, "If I had her, finally, something would be right in my lousy life. If I had her, life would have meaning. If I had her, it would *fix* things." If he found his one true love, life would finally be okay. All the longings of the human heart for significance, for security, and for meaning—he had no other object for them—they were all fixed on Rachel.

Jacob was somewhat unusual for his time. Cultural historians will tell you that in ancient times people didn't generally marry for love (that is actually a relatively recent phenomenon). They married for status. Nevertheless, he is not rare today. Ernest Becker was a secular man, an atheist, who won the Pulitzer Prize in the 1970s for his book *The Denial of Death*. In the book, he talks about how secular people deal with the fact that they don't believe in God. He says that one of the main ways our secular culture has dealt with the God vacuum is through apocalyptic sex and romance. Our secular culture has loaded its desire for transcendence into romance and love. Talking about the modern secular person, he says:

> He still needed to feel heroic, to know that his life mattered in the scheme of things. . . . He still had to merge himself with some higher, self-absorbing meaning, in trust and gratitude. . . . If he no longer had God, how was he to do this? One of the first ways that occurred to him, as [Otto] Rank saw, was the "romantic solution." . . . The self-glorification that he needed in his innermost nature he now looked for in the love partner. The love partner becomes the divine ideal within which to fulfill one's life. . . .
>
> After all, what is it that we want when we elevate the love partner to the position of God? We want redemption—nothing less. We want to be rid of our faults, of our feelings of nothingness. *We want to be justified*, to know that our creation has not been in vain.[3]

That is exactly what Jacob did. And that is what people are doing all over the place. That is what our culture is begging us to do—to

3. Ernest Becker, *The Denial of Death* (New York: Free Press, 1973), 160, 167 (emphasis added).

load all of the deepest needs of our hearts for significance, security, and transcendence into romance and love, into finding that one true love. *That will fix my lousy life!*

Let me tell you something you notice when you live in New York City. It is a tough town; everybody looks so cool and pulled together. But the amount of money people spend on their appearance shows they are desperate. They cannot imagine living without *apocalyptic* romance and love. The human longing for one true love has always been around, but in our culture now, it has been magnified to an astounding degree. But where does it lead?

The Disillusionment That Comes

Secondly, let's look at the disillusionment and devastation that almost always accompanies a search for that one true love. We begin with Laban's plot. Laban knew that Jacob offered to serve seven years for Rachel. He knew what that meant. At that time, when you wanted to marry someone, you paid the father a bride-price, and it was somewhere around thirty or forty shekels, maybe forty-five. Robert Alter says that a month's wages was equal to one-and-a-half shekels, and therefore, you can see that Jacob, right out of the box, is absolutely lovesick. He is a horrible bargainer; he has immediately offered three to four times the normal bride-price. Laban knew he had him. He knew this man was vulnerable.

Commentators say there are indications in the text that Laban immediately came up with a plan, realizing he could get even more out of this deal. Notice the conversation between Jacob and Laban. The text says, "Jacob was in love with Rachel and said, 'I'll work for you seven years in return for your younger daughter Rachel'" (v. 18). Look at how Laban responds. He never says, "Yes"! He does not say, "Yes, seven years. It is a deal." No! He says, "It's better that I give her to you than to some other man" (v. 19). Jacob wants it to be a yes, so he hears a yes. But it is not a yes. Laban is just saying, "Yea, okay, if you want to marry Rachel, it is a good idea."

Seven years pass; now Jacob says, "Give me my wife." As customary, there is a great feast. In the middle of the feast, the bride is brought heavily veiled to the groom. She was given to him, and he took her into her tent. He was inebriated, as was also the custom;

and in that dark tent, Jacob lay with her. The text tells us, "When morning came, there was Leah!" (v. 25). Jacob looked and discovered that he had married Leah, and he had had sex with Leah, and he had consummated the marriage with Leah. Jacob, rightfully angry, goes to Laban and says, "What is this you have done to me? I served you for Rachel, didn't I? Why have you deceived me?" (v. 25). Laban replies that it is customary for the older girl to be married before the younger girl.

I must say I have read this text for thirty years or more and I have never understood why Jacob basically says, "Oh, okay." I have never figured it out. He is obviously angry and the situation is absolutely ridiculous. Why doesn't Jacob kill him? Why doesn't he throttle him? Again, Robert Alter is very helpful here. He suggests something that I think is rather profound. First of all, what Laban literally says is: "It is not the custom *here* to put the younger before the older."

Second, Alter points out that when Jacob said, "Why have you deceived me?" the word translated "deceived" is the same Hebrew word that was used in chapter 27 to describe what Jacob did to Isaac. Alter says (this is surmise, but what surmise!) that it must have occurred to Jacob that Laban had only done to him what he had done to his father. In the dark, he thought he was touching Rachel, as his father in the dark of his blindness had thought he was touching Esau. Alter then quotes an ancient rabbinical commentator who imagines the conversation the next day between Jacob and Leah. Jacob says to Leah: "I called out 'Rachel' in the dark and you answered. Why did you do that to me?" And Leah says to him, "Your father called out 'Esau' in the dark and you answered. Why did you do that to him?" Fury dies on his lips. Cut to the quick. Suddenly the evil he has done has come home to Jacob. And he sees what it is like to be manipulated and deceived, and meekly he picks up and works another seven years.

We leave Jacob in his devastation (I don't have a better word for it), and then we see what it has done to Leah. Now, who is Leah? We are told that Leah is the older daughter, but the only detail we are given about her is that she has weak eyes. Nobody quite knows what "weak eyes" means; some commentators have assumed it means she has bad eyesight. But the text does not say that Leah had weak eyes, *but Rachel could see a long way.* Weakness probably means cross-eyed; it could mean something unsightly. But here is the point: Leah was particularly unattractive, and she had to live all of her life in the shadow of her sister who was absolutely stunning. As a result, Laban knew no one was ever going to marry her or offer any money for her. He wondered how he was going to get rid of her, how he was going to unload her. And then he saw his chance, he saw an opening, and he did it. And now the girl that Laban, her father, did not want has been given to a husband who doesn't want her either. She is the girl nobody wants.

Leah has a hollow in her heart every bit as big as the hollow in Jacob's heart. Now she begins to do to Jacob what Jacob had done to Rachel and what Isaac had done to Esau. She set her heart on Jacob. You see the evil and the pathology in these families just ricocheting around again and again from generation to generation.

The last verses here are some of the most plaintive I have ever read in the Bible (most English translations tell you a little about what the words actually mean). Leah gave birth to her first child, a boy, and she named him Reuben. Reuben means "to see" and she thought, "Now maybe my husband will see me; maybe I won't be invisible anymore." But it wasn't true. So she had a second son, and she named him Simeon, which has to do with hearing: "Now maybe my husband will finally listen to me." But he didn't. She had a third son and named him Levi, which means "to be attached," and she said, "Maybe finally my husband's heart will be attached to me."

What was she doing? She was trying to get an identity through traditional family values. Having sons, especially in those days, was the best way to do that; but it was not working. She had set her heart, all of her hopes and dreams, on her husband. She thought, "If I have babies and if I have sons and my husband loves me, then finally something will be fixed in my lousy life." Instead, she was just going down into hell. And the text says—it is sort of like the summary statement—Jacob loved Rachel more than Leah. That meant she was condemned every single day. This is what I mean by hell—every single day she was condemned to see the man she most longed for in the arms of the one in whose shadow she has lived all of her life. Every day was like another knife in the heart.

All we see here is devastation, right? No, that is actually not the way the text ends. But before we look at how the text ends, let me field two objections and draw two lessons. The first objection has to do with all these ancient practices. Some people who read the text or listen to a sermon on it are thinking, *Why are you telling me this story—men buying and selling women, primogeniture, sexual slavery—what is this about? I am offended by this kind of old primitive culture. I know they existed, but thank goodness we don't live in a culture like that anymore. Why do we have to know about it?*

First, it is important to see (and this comes from what Robert Alter says), if you read the book of Genesis, and you think it is condoning primogeniture, polygamy, and bride purchase—if you think it is condoning these things, you have not yet learned how to read. Because in absolutely every single place where you see polygamy or primogeniture, it always wreaks devastation. It never works out. All you ever see is the misery these patriarchal institutions cause in families. Alter says if you think the book of Genesis is promoting those things, you have no idea what is being said. He says these stories are *subversive* to all those ancient patriarchal institutions. Just read!

You might also be thinking, *Thank goodness we don't live in a culture in which a woman's value is based on her looks. Thank goodness we don't live in a culture where a woman looks in a mirror and says, "Look at me! I am a size 4, I can get a rich husband." Hundreds of years ago, people used to do that but nobody does that anymore.* Really? I am sorry, I shouldn't be sarcastic, but what in the world makes you think that we are in a less brutal culture? We are and we aren't. Besides that, what the Bible says about the human heart is always true, it is always abiding. If anything, what we are saying is more true today than it was before.

The second objection people have has to do with the moral of the story. They ask, "Where are all the spiritual heroes in this text? Who am I supposed to be emulating? Who is the good guy? What is the moral of the story? I don't see any! What is going on here?"

The answer is: That is absolutely correct. You are starting to get it. You are starting to get the point of the Bible. What do I mean? The Bible doesn't give us a god at the top of a moral ladder saying, "Look at the people who have found God through their great performance and their moral record. Be like them!" Of course not! Instead, over and over again, the Bible gives us absolutely weak people who don't seek the grace they need and who don't deserve the grace they get. They don't appreciate it after they get it, and they continue to screw up and abuse it even after they have it. And yet, the grace keeps coming! The Bible is not about a god who gives us accounts of moral heroes. It is about grace, and that is what this story is about. So what do we learn from this story? Is there any moral? I wouldn't put it that way, but here are two things I would like you to see:

First, we learn that through all of life there runs a ground note of cosmic disappointment. You are never going to lead a wise life, no matter who you are, unless you understand that. Here is Jacob, and he says, "If I can just get Rachel, everything will be okay." And he goes to bed with someone whom he thinks is Rachel, and then, literally, the Hebrew says, "But in the morning, behold, it was Leah." What does this show us? Listen, I love Leah; I really do. I have been thinking about this text for a long time, and I love her and I want to protect her, so I hope you don't think I am being mean to her in what I am trying to say. But I want you to know that—when you get married, no matter how great you think that marriage is going to be; when you get into a career, no matter how great you think that career is going to be; when you go off to seminary, no matter how much you think it is going to make you into a man or woman of God—*in the morning, it is always Leah!* You think you are going to bed with Rachel, and in the morning, it is always Leah. Nobody has ever said this better than C. S. Lewis in *Mere Christianity*:

> Most people, if they have really learned to look into their own hearts, would know that they do want, and want acutely, something that cannot be had in this world. There are all sorts of things in this world that offer to give it to you, but they never quite keep their promise. The longings which arise in us when we first fall in love, or first think of some foreign country, or first take up some subject that excites us, are longings which no marriage, no travel, no learning, can really satisfy. I am not now speaking of what would be ordinarily called unsuccessful marriages, or holidays, or learned careers. I am speaking of the best possible ones. There was something we have

grasped at, in that first moment of longing, which just fades away in the reality. I think everyone knows what I mean. The wife may be a good wife, and the hotels and scenery may have been excellent, and chemistry may be a very interesting job: but something has evaded us.[4]

You have got to understand that it is always Leah! Why? Because if you get married, if you have families, if you go into the ministry, and say that "finally this is going to fix my life" (you don't really think you are doing it until you do it)—those things will never do what you think they will do. In the morning, it is always Leah. If you get married, and in any way do as Jacob does and put that kind of weight on the person you are marrying, you are going to crush him or her. You are going to kill each other. You are going to think you have gone to bed with Rachel, but you get up and it is Leah.

As time goes on, eventually you are going to know that this is the case; that everything disappoints, that there is a note of cosmic disappointment and disillusionment in everything, in all the things into which we most put our hopes. When you finally find that out, there are four things you can do. One, you can blame the things and drop them and go try and get new ones, better ones. That is the fool's way. The second thing you can do is blame yourself and beat yourself up and say, "I have somehow been a failure. I see everybody else happy. I don't know why I am not happy. There is something wrong with me." So you blame yourself and you become a self-hater. Third, you can blame the world and get cynical and hard. You say, "Curses on the entire opposite sex" or whatever, in which case you dehumanize yourself. Lastly, you can, as C. S Lewis says at the end of his great chapter on hope, change the entire focus of your life. He concludes, "If I find in myself a desire which no experience in this world can satisfy, the most probable explanation is that I was made for another world [something supernatural and eternal]."[5]

Second, we see that both the liberal mindset and the conservative mindset are wrong when it comes to romance, sex, and love. Neither serves us well. In fact, you can almost see it in Jacob and Leah. Jacob,

4. C. S. Lewis, *Mere Christianity* (various editions), Book III, ch. 10, "Hope."
5. Ibid., "Hope."

with a liberal mindset, is after an apocalyptic hookup. He says, "Give me my wife! I want sex!" He actually says that. On the other hand, here is Leah, and what is she doing? She is the conservative. She is having babies. She is not out having a career. She is trying to find her identity in being a wife—"Now my husband will love me."

Guess what? They are both wrong. They are not going anywhere. Their lives are a mess. That is the reason why Ernest Becker says so beautifully, "No human relationship can bear the burden of god-hood. . . . However much we may idealize and idolize him [the love partner], he inevitably reflects earthly decay and imperfection. And as he is our ideal measure of value, this imperfection falls back upon us. If your partner is your 'All' then any shortcoming in him becomes a major threat to *you*."[6] As Becker said, what we want when we elevate the love partner to the position of God is to be rid of our faults, to be justified, to know our existence has not been in vain. We are after redemption. He then adds, "Needless to say, human partners can't do this."[7] You might think that is pretty obvious; but we do not believe it. We thought the Bible was a source of family values. Well, it is, in a sense, but how realistic it is! So what are we going to do? We are all creatures of our culture. We have this drive in us for one true love. What are we going to do with it? Here is the answer.

What We Can Do about This Longing

I want you to see what God does *in* Leah and *for* Leah. Leah is the first person to get it; she does begin to see what you are supposed to do. Look first at what God does in her. As we have said, every time she has a child, she puts all of her hopes in her husband now loving her. And yet, one of the things scholars notice that is very curious is that even though she is clearly making a functional idol out of her husband and her family, she is calling on *the Lord*. She doesn't talk about God in some general way or invoke the name Elohim. She uses the name *Yahweh*. In verse 32, it says, "Leah became pregnant and gave birth to a son. She named him Reuben,

6. Becker, *Denial of Death*, 166.
7. Ibid., 167.

for she said, 'It is because *the* LORD [Yahweh] has seen my misery.'"
How does she know about Yahweh?

Elohim was the generic word for God back then. All cultures at
that time had some general idea of God or gods; they were gods at
the top of a ladder, and you had to get up to the top through rituals
or through transformations of consciousness or moral performance.
Everyone understood God in that sense, but Yahweh was different.
Yahweh was the God who came down the ladder, the one who
entered into a personal covenantal relationship and intervened to
save. Certainly they didn't know all he was going to do, but Abraham and Isaac knew something about it, and Jacob would have
known about it as well. It is interesting that Leah must have learned
about Yahweh from Jacob. Even though she is still in the grip of her
functional idolatry, somehow she is trying, she is calling out, she is
reaching out to *a God of grace.* She has grasped the concept.

You might say that she has got a theology of sorts, as advanced
as it was at the time, but she is having trouble connecting it. She
is calling him the Lord, and yet she is treating him like a "god."
Do you follow me? She is saying, "God can help me save myself
through childbearing. God can help me save myself by getting my
husband's love." So she is using God, and yet she does not call him
God [*Elohim*]; she calls him Lord [*Yahweh*]. She is beginning to get
it, and what is intriguing is that, at the very end, something happens.
The first time she gives birth she says, "Now maybe my husband
will see me. Now maybe my husband will love me." And when she
gives birth to her third son, she says, "Now maybe my husband will
be attached to me."

Finally, it says that she conceived for the fourth time, and when
she gave birth to Judah, she said, "This time!" Isn't that defiant? It is
totally different; no mention of husband, no mention of child. There
is some kind of breakthrough. She says, "*This time* I will praise the
LORD." At that point, she has finally taken her heart's deepest hopes
off of the old way, off of her husband and her children, and she has
put them in the Lord.

Here is what I believe is going on. Jacob and Laban had stolen
Leah's life, but when she stopped giving her heart to a good thing
that she had turned into an *ultimate* thing and gave it to the Lord, she

got her life back. May I respectfully ask you: What good thing in your life are you treating as an ultimate thing? What do you need to stop giving your heart to if you are going to get your life back? There are a lot of things I am not certain about, but I am absolutely certain that everybody in this room has got something. Do you know what it is? If you have no idea, you need to think about it. Something happened to Leah; God did something in her. There was a breakthrough. She began to understand what you are supposed to do with your desire for one true love. She turned her heart toward the only real beauty, the only real lover who can satisfy those cosmic needs.

But we shouldn't just look at what God did in her. We have to also look at what God has done *for* her—because God has done something for her. I believe that she had some consciousness, although it might have been semi-consciousness or just intuition, that there was something special about this last child. It would probably be reading too much into the text to say she understood, but I believe she sensed that God had done something for her. And he had. The writer of Genesis knows what God had done. This child is Judah, and who is Judah? The writer of Genesis tells us in chapter 49 that it is through Judah that Shiloh will come, and it is through Shiloh that the King will come. This is the line! This is the Messianic line! God has come to the girl that nobody wanted, the unloved, the unwanted, and made her the mother of Jesus! This is the mother of Jesus—not beautiful Rachel, but the homely one, the unwanted one, the unloved one.

Why did God do that? Does he just like the underdog? He did it because of his person and because of his work. First, because of his person. It says that when the Lord saw that Leah was not loved, *he* loved her. God is saying, "I am the real bridegroom. I am the husband of the husbandless. I am the father of the fatherless." What does that mean? He is attracted to the people that the world is not attracted to. He loves the unwanted. He loves the unattractive. He loves the weak, the ones the world doesn't want to be like. God says, "If nobody else is going to be the spouse of Leah, I will be her spouse."

Guess what? It is not just those of you without spouses who need to see God as your ultimate spouse, but those of us with spouses have got to see God as our ultimate spouse as well. You have to demote the person you are married to out of first place in your heart to second place behind God or you will end up killing each other. You will put all of your freight, all the weight of all your hopes, on that person. And of course, they are human beings, they are sinners, just like you are. God says you must see him as what he is: the great bridegroom, the spouse for the spouseless. He is not just a king and we are the subjects; he is not just a shepherd and we are the sheep. He is a husband and we are his lovers. He loves us! He is ravished with us—even those of us whom no one else is ravished with; *especially* those of us whom no one else is ravished with. That is his person. But that is not all.

The second reason why he goes after Leah and not Rachel, why he makes the girl who nobody wanted into the mother of Jesus, the bearer of the Messianic line, the bearer of salvation to the world, is not just that he likes the underdog, but because that is the gospel. When God came to earth in Jesus Christ, he was the son of Leah. Oh yes, he was! He became the man nobody wanted. He was born in a manger. He had no beauty that we should desire him. He came to his own and his own received him not. And at the end, nobody wanted him. Everybody abandoned him. Even his Father in heaven didn't want him. Jesus cried out on the cross: "My God, my God, why have you forsaken me?"

Why did he become Leah's son? Why did he become the man nobody wanted? For you and for me! Here is the gospel: God did not save us *in spite of* the weakness that he experienced as a human being but *through* it. And you don't actually get that salvation into your life through your strength; it is only for those who admit they are weak. And if you cannot admit that you are a hopeless moral failure and a sinner and that you are absolutely lost and have no hope apart from the sheer grace of God, then you are not weak enough for Leah and her son and the great salvation that God has brought into the world.

God chose Leah because he is saying, "This is how salvation works. This is the upside-down way that my people will live, at least in relationship to the world, when they receive my salvation." Now the way up is down. The way to become rich is to give your money away. The way to power is to serve. God, when he came to earth, was the son of Leah. God made Leah, the girl nobody wanted, into the mother of Jesus. Why? Because he chooses the foolish things to shame the wise; he chooses the weak things to shame the strong; he chooses even the things that are not to bring to nothing the things that are, so that no one will boast in his presence (1 Cor. 1:27–29).

In conclusion, let me give you a couple of practical applications. *First*, if there is anyone with a Laban in their life right now, don't be bitter and don't beat them up. Don't let them take advantage of you either if you can; but remember, God can use that person in your life to make you better if you don't become bitter.

Second, are you somebody who has been rejected, betrayed, maybe recently divorced and you didn't want to be? Are you a Leah? Remember, God knows what it is like to be rejected. He didn't just love Leah, but he actually became Leah. He became the son of Leah. He came to his own and his own received him not. He understands rejection, and if anything, he is, from what we can tell in the Scripture, attracted to people in your condition. It is his nature, so don't worry. He knows and he cares.

Third, please don't let marriage throw you. I have been saying this all along: in the morning, it will always be Leah. And if you understand that, it will make some of you less desperate in your marriage-seeking, and it will make some of you less angry at your spouse for his or her imperfections. Honestly, you have got to understand that.

Last, you may believe you have screwed up your life; that your life is on plan B. You should have done this or that, and now it is too late. Think about it: Should Jacob have deceived Isaac and Esau? No. Should Isaac have shown the favoritism that turned Jacob into a liar? No. Everybody sinned. There are no excuses. They shouldn't have done what they did. They blew up their lives. But if those things hadn't happened, would Jacob ever have met the love of his life, Rachel? Jesus Christ, who is a result of Jacob's having to flee to the other side of the Fertile Crescent, isn't plan B! You can't mess up your life. You can't screw up God's plan for you. You will find that no matter how much you do to mess it up, all you are doing is fulfilling his destiny for you. That does not mean what they did was okay. The devastation and the unhappiness and the misery that happens in your life because of your sins are your fault. You are responsible, you shouldn't do them; and yet, God is going to work through you. Those two things are together. It is an antinomy, a paradox. Remember, it is never too late for God to work in your life! Never! You can't put yourself on plan B. Go to him. Start over now. Say it: *"This time, no matter what else I have done, I will praise the Lord!"*

3

LORD AND SERVANT

Genesis 43

Brian Vos

Introduction

I remember receiving it in the mail: a gift from Westminster Seminary California, a small green book, only ninety pages in length, entitled *Called to the Ministry*.[1] It was my junior year in college; I was considering seminary, and it was the first time I heard the name of Dr. Edmund P. Clowney. After reading the book, and with much prayer, I was convinced that the Lord was indeed calling me to the ministry of the Word and sacraments; I was also convinced that I wanted to study at the seminary where Dr. Clowney taught.

Approximately two years later, my wife and I moved to California to begin my seminary training at Westminster. In my first year I audited a class of Dr. Clowney's entitled Preaching Christ in the Pentateuch. Though Dr. Clowney never made it much beyond the

---

1. Edmund P. Clowney, *Called to the Ministry* (Phillipsburg, NJ: Presbyterian & Reformed, 1964).

opening chapters of Exodus, it was a joy to hear him unfold the riches of Christ in the stories of Noah, Abraham, Isaac, Jacob, Joseph, and Moses. How often my heart burned within me as he opened God's Word! This was to become a common—though no less joyful—experience in each of the classes I took with Dr. Clowney. My second year preaching class with Dr. Clowney was perhaps the most difficult course I took with him, yet also the most rewarding. Each time a student "preached," Dr. Clowney would offer his critique. More often than not, his comments would slowly turn into a sermon itself. That was when I learned the most. Here was a man whose heart was so gripped by the glory of our Lord and Savior Jesus Christ, and so "at home" in the biblical text, he could hardly offer his evaluation without unfolding the mystery of Jesus Christ. During those times I would begin by furiously taking notes, trying to capture everything he was saying so as not to lose it. Inevitably, however, I would finally put my pen down and just sit and listen as my heart was drawn to Jesus Christ once again.

The last time I heard Dr. Clowney speak was at a conference the student council put together in his honor. I can still see him standing on the stage, a somewhat small and diminutive figure; I can still hear him speaking with a weak, but ever-so-gracious voice; I can still feel the energetic silence of the audience, hanging on his every word: Dr. Clowney was taking us from Genesis to Revelation and unfolding the mystery of Christ in the history of redemption, and my heart was burning within me. His time was over too quickly. Dr. Clowney always left me wanting to know more of Christ, and for that I am grateful.

It is my hope and prayer that this sermon exhibits something of his legacy. I preached this sermon at Trinity United Reformed Church of Grand Rapids, Michigan, on February 13, 2005, as part of the final installment of a series on Genesis. I had divided the series so that the last section we considered together was the story of Joseph, found in Genesis 37–50. As we made our way through these familiar chapters, we marveled at the glories of Jesus Christ found in them. How brightly those glories shine in Genesis 43! We had celebrated the sacrament of the Lord's Supper together during the morning service, and then had the privilege of turning to Genesis 43 in the evening, enabling us to see the wonders of grace in terms of our Lord's exalted service to us, as it is so poignantly demonstrated in the story of Joseph, the exalted "lord of the land" who took servings to his sinful brothers.

Dr. Clowney always taught us to preach vividly, giving due heed to the narrative in its own context, as well as that of the entire Scripture, centering upon Christ. In Genesis 43 we certainly see the riches of Jesus Christ and his ministry to us. In the broader context of the Joseph story, however, we see not only the parallels between Joseph and Jesus, but also the Lord working mightily in Joseph's life, conforming him to Jesus, the true Lord and Servant.

Thus, the Lord of the Word calls us to himself in the Word of the Lord. He calls sinners to find forgiveness, mercy, grace, peace, comfort, and joy in him. He calls saints to continue to feast upon him, thereby growing in grace. Such transformation comes only by God's grace, and that grace is found only in Jesus Christ, the exalted Lord of glory, who came not to be served, but to serve, and to give his life a ransom for many.

In the course of my ministry I have loaned my copy of Dr. Clowney's "small green book" to a number of young men considering the ministry and seminary. The last time I did so, I did not receive it back; and I don't remember to whom I loaned it. When I wanted to obtain a copy of the book once again, I went to the used section of a local Christian bookstore, and was delighted to find a copy there. I opened the inside cover and was surprised to find a label affixed which read:

This book provided by:
WESTMINSTER SEMINARY IN CALIFORNIA
1725 Bear Valley Pkwy
Escondido, CA 92027

I don't think it was my original copy, but I do think Dr. Clowney would have grinned to see his book, and his ministry, still being used. May his service continue to be used of the Lord to lead many into the ministry that the glories of Jesus Christ, our Lord and Servant, may be published abroad.

The Scripture (Genesis 43)[2]

Now the famine was severe in the land. And it came to pass, when they had eaten up the grain which they had brought from Egypt, that their father said to them, "Go back, buy us a little food."

But Judah spoke to him, saying, "The man solemnly warned us, saying, 'You shall not see my face unless your brother is with you.' If you send our brother with us, we will go down and buy you food. But if you will not send him, we will not go down; for the man said to us, 'You shall not see my face unless your brother is with you.'"

And Israel said, "Why did you deal so wrongfully with me as to tell the man whether you had still another brother?"

But they said, "The man asked us pointedly about ourselves and our family, saying 'Is your father still alive? Have you another brother?' And we told him according to these words. Could we possibly have known that he would say, 'Bring your brother down'?"

Then Judah said to Israel his father, "Send the lad with me, and we will arise and go, that we may live and not die, both we and you and also our little ones. I myself will be surety for him; from my hand you shall require him. If I do not bring him back to you and set him before you, then let me bear the blame forever. For if we had not lingered, surely by now we would have returned this second time."

And their father Israel said to them, "If it must be so, then do this: Take some of the best fruits of the land in your vessels and carry down a present for the man—a little balm and a little honey, spices, and myrrh, pistachio nuts and almonds. Take double money in your hand, and take back in your hand the money that was returned in the mouth of your sacks; perhaps it was an oversight. Take your brother also, and arise, go back to the man. And may God Almighty give you mercy before the man, that he may release your other brother and Benjamin. If I am bereaved, I am bereaved!"

So the men took that present and Benjamin, and they took double money in their hand, and arose and went down to Egypt; and they stood before Joseph. When Joseph saw Benjamin with them, he said to the steward of his house, "Take these men to my home, and slaughter an animal and make ready; for these men will dine with me at noon." Then the man did as Joseph ordered, and the man brought the men into Joseph's house.

2. Scripture citations in this sermon are from the NKJV.

Now the men were afraid because they were brought into Joseph's house; and they said, "It is because of the money, which was returned in our sacks the first time, that we are brought in, so that he may make a case against us and seize us, to take us as slaves with our donkeys."

When they drew near to the steward of Joseph's house, they talked with him at the door of the house, and said, "O sir, we indeed came down the first time to buy food; but it happened, when we came to the encampment, that we opened our sacks, and there, each man's money was in the mouth of his sack, our money in full weight; so we have brought it back in our hand. And we have brought down other money in our hands to buy food. We do not know who put our money in our sacks."

But he said, "Peace be with you, do not be afraid. Your God and the God of your father has given you treasure in your sacks; I had your money." Then he brought Simeon out to them.

So the man brought the men into Joseph's house and gave them water, and they washed their feet; and he gave their donkeys feed. Then they made the present ready for Joseph's coming at noon, for they heard that they would eat bread there.

And when Joseph came home, they brought him the present which was in their hand into the house, and bowed down before him to the earth. Then he asked them about their well-being, and said, "Is your father well, the old man of whom you spoke? Is he still alive?"

And they answered, "Your servant our father is in good health; he is still alive." And they bowed their heads down and prostrated themselves.

Then he lifted his eyes and saw his brother Benjamin, his mother's son, and said, "Is this your younger brother of whom you spoke to me?" And he said, "God be gracious to you, my son." Now his heart yearned for his brother; so Joseph made haste and sought somewhere to weep. And he went into his chamber and wept there. Then he washed his face and came out; and he restrained himself, and said, "Serve the bread."

So they set him a place by himself, and them by themselves, and the Egyptians who ate with him by themselves; because the Egyptians could not eat food with the Hebrews, for that is an abomination to the Egyptians. And they sat before him, the firstborn according to his birthright and the youngest according to his youth; and

the men looked in astonishment at one another. Then he took servings to them from before him, but Benjamin's serving was five times
as much as any of theirs. So they drank and were merry with him.

The Sermon

It must have been a miserable time in the lives of Joseph's brothers.
With their stomachs empty and growling, and no food left in their
own land, they made the long, hot, grueling trip down to Egypt to
buy grain. While in Egypt, they were treated harshly. The lord of
the land, who sat at the right hand of the mighty and exalted Pha-
raoh himself, accused them of being spies. He imprisoned them,
and even bound their brother Simeon, telling them he would release him only if they returned with their youngest brother. Then
Joseph would know they were not spies.

With no other options before them, the brothers proceeded to
purchase some grain. How heavy their sacks must have seemed as
they loaded them upon their donkeys, the false accusations still ringing in their ears, the sight of their brother Simeon in bonds replaying
in their minds. Under such weight they began their journey back to
Canaan, a land now devoid of milk and honey. Along the way, one
of them opened his sack to give his donkey feed, only to discover
his money in the mouth of his sack. Their hearts failed them, and
in their fear they cried out to one another, "What is this that God
has done to us?" (42:28). It seemed to them that God was against
them, perhaps even punishing them. What would lead them to think
such a thing? A guilty conscience. They were struck with guilt over
something they had done years before. They had already admitted
as much to one another: "We are truly guilty concerning our brother,
for we saw the anguish of his soul when he pleaded with us, and we
would not hear; therefore this distress has come upon us" (42:21).
The sin, the guilt, and the shame of selling their brother Joseph into
slavery years ago were coming back to torment them.

It was not only the brothers, however, who felt the burden of
these things. When they finally returned to the dry and barren land
of Canaan and reported all that had happened to their father, it was
Jacob who said, "You have bereaved me: Joseph is no more, Simeon
is no more, and you want to take Benjamin. All these things are

against me!" (42:36). Under this miserable weight, they sat down to fill their empty stomachs and silence their growling bellies with the grain they had bought in Egypt. How unpleasant every meal must have been. Each spoonful served to remind them that Simeon remained bound in Egypt. Each mouthful told them Simeon could not come back unless Benjamin returned with them. With every meal, their grain was running out. But Jacob refused to be bereft of yet another son (42:38). It must have been a miserable time in the lives of Joseph's brothers.

Their misery only increased as they rationed what little grain was left. All too quickly, the portions became smaller and smaller, their stomachs emptier and emptier, the growling of their bellies louder and louder. Finally, the last supper came, the grain was gone, and the famine in the land was as severe as ever. When the groans of his empty stomach became more than he could bear, Jacob finally said to his sons, "Go back, buy us a little food." If they did nothing, they would all die of starvation. The only option left is to go back to Egypt and buy some more grain from the lord of the land.

There's just one problem, and Judah reminds his father of it. "The lord of the land strictly warned us that we could not see his face unless our brother was with us. Send Benjamin, and we'll go. Refuse to send him, and we all stay here and die in our misery." Jacob then accuses his sons in words wrought with irony: "Why did you deal so wrongfully with me as to tell the man whether you had still another brother?" (v. 6). Jacob charges his sons with wronging him by telling the lord of the land about his youngest son. That irony, unbeknownst to Jacob, was not lost on Judah. Even as he defended their actions regarding Benjamin, his conscience told him there was no defense for what they had done to Joseph so many years ago. Though the brothers may not have wronged their father concerning Benjamin (how were they to know that the lord of the land would require his coming?), they had wronged him terribly concerning Joseph years ago. What they had done was sinful, shameful, unkind; it left them all feeling the pains of a guilty conscience.

From his troubled conscience, Judah responds, "Send the lad with me, and we will arise and go, that we may live and not die, both we and you and also our little ones. I myself will be surety for him;

from my hand you shall require him. If I do not bring him back to you and set him before you, then let me bear the blame forever. For if we had not lingered, surely by now we would have returned this second time" (vv. 8–10). Judah, who once would not give his own son to his daughter-in-law Tamar for fear of losing him (Genesis 38), now offers himself as surety for Jacob's son.[3]

To this Jacob finally agrees. Recognizing the potential disfavor of the lord of the land, Jacob seeks to appease him with gifts. He remembered his tactics with Esau so many years ago. He told his sons to take down with them, as a present for the lord of the land (who, as lord of the land, certainly didn't need anything at all!) a little balm and a little honey, spices and myrrh, pistachio nuts and almonds, and also double money in their hands, hoping that the money in their sacks was just an oversight. Last of all, he gave them Benjamin, saying, "May God Almighty give you mercy before the man, that he may release your other brother and Benjamin. If I am bereaved, I am bereaved!"

On the basis of this speech, Jacob has sometimes been viewed here as a stoic fatalist. To view him as such is to miss not only God's working in his life, but also one of his greatest statements of faith. He appeals to God Almighty, *El Shaddai*, consigning himself and his family to the providence of the Lord, recognizing that however the Lord deals with them, it will be for his purposes and according to his mercy and grace. Significantly, Jacob is referred to here by his new name, *Israel*, the very name God gave to him on that night in which he wrestled with the Lord at Peniel (Gen. 32:22–32). There the Lord wounded Jacob's hip so that he could not prevail in his own strength, and then warned him as day was about to break, "Let me go!" To this, Jacob responded, "I will not let you go unless you bless me!" The Lord then asked his name, to which he had to respond: "My name is Jacob! Deceiver. Supplanter. Sinner. And I now realize that my only hope is you." There the Lord changed Jacob's name to Israel, for he struggled with the Lord and prevailed. That night Jacob saw the Lord face to face and his life was preserved. Only in

---

3. A beautiful message in the story of Judah begins to take shape here, but it is not fully developed until Genesis 44:18–34, where Judah, true to his word, actually intercedes on Benjamin's behalf, offering himself as a slave in the place of Benjamin.

weakness did Jacob prevail with the Lord.[4] Thus the Lord called him "Israel."

Now Jacob is called Israel again. Now he learns the lesson again: he must rely entirely upon the Lord. The only way he can save Benjamin is by letting him go. The only way he can save his wicked sons, who have already bereaved him, is by giving up his beloved son. With Joseph it was not by choice, with Benjamin it is. He can do no better than to consign the whole matter to the Lord of providence.

Against the backdrop of their father's statement of faith, and with Benjamin alongside them, the brothers depart for Egypt, that they might stand once again before the lord of the land. The brothers, however, did not share their father's confidence in the providence of the Lord. Even as they made this second journey to Egypt, their sins rose up against them; their guilty consciences accused them all the more. How would the Lord of providence, who seemed to be against them, orchestrate these events? How would the lord of the land, who had treated them harshly, receive them? Would his fury be aroused against them due to the money in their sacks? Would he let Simeon go? What would he do with Benjamin? Would he allow them to return to Canaan? Would he let them live? What fear must have gripped their hearts as they made their way down to Egypt! How their guilty consciences must have plagued them as they went to stand again in the presence of the lord of the land!

When Joseph saw them once again, and Benjamin with them, he did not respond to them in derision; he did not speak to them in his wrath, nor distress them in his deep displeasure. Instead, he commanded that they be brought to his home that they might enjoy a noontime meal with him. How their roles have reversed! Years before, it was the brothers who ate a meal, while Joseph pleaded with them in anguish from the pit (Gen. 37:25; 42:21). Now as Joseph brings them to his house for a meal, they are the ones in anguish.

Once they entered his home, the brothers' fear could be held back no more:

4. Cf. Edmund P. Clowney, *Preaching Christ in All of Scripture* (Wheaton, IL: Crossway, 2003), 87–94.

Now the men were afraid because they were brought into Joseph's house; and they said, "It is because of the money, which was returned in our sacks the first time, that we are brought in, so that he may make a case against us, to take us as slaves with our donkeys."

When they drew near to the steward of Joseph's house, they talked with him at the door of the house, and said, "O sir, we indeed came down the first time to buy food; but it happened, when we came to the encampment, that we opened our sacks, and there, each man's money was in the mouth of his sack, our money in full weight; so we have brought it back in our hand. And we have brought down other money in our hands to buy food. We do not know who put our money in our sacks." (Gen. 43:18–22)

Joseph's overture of grace—a meal with the lord of the land in his home—was met with fear and suspicion. Such is the power of a guilty conscience.

The overtures of grace, however, are not easily deterred. The brothers are gripped with fear; Joseph shows more grace, more mercy. His steward said to the brothers, "Peace be with you, do not be afraid. Your God and the God of your father has given you treasure in your sacks; I had your money . . ." (v. 23). Certainly Joseph had informed the steward of the whole matter and instructed him to deal graciously and mercifully with his brothers. His intent was to soothe their guilty consciences with the healing balm of grace.

In fact, Joseph added grace upon grace, orchestrating each action so as to bring healing to their poor souls. After this initial mercy, he brought Simeon out to them unbound and unharmed. (How could he be harmed by a lord so gracious as Joseph?) He gave them water to wash their feet—the soothing and cleansing effect of the water for their feet was intended to have the same effect upon their souls. He also gave their donkeys feed. The brothers had been afraid that they would be taken as slaves together with their donkeys. But fear is met with grace. Instead of bonds, they are given water; instead of slavery, even their donkeys are given feed. What relief it must have brought to the brothers to receive such mercy and grace!

Yet while the healing balm of grace is a gift, it is not easily received as such. Joseph's brothers can scarcely bring themselves to trust such kindness, such mercy, such grace. They still want to earn the favor of the lord of the land; they still want to appease him with something from their own hands. Thus they present their gifts to him, bowing down to the earth before him.

Joseph beholds his brothers bowing down before him and recalls the dreams of long ago. But he does not respond in haughtiness and pride. He does not use his position of authority to seek vengeance upon those who mocked him, scorned him, abused him, and rejected him. On the contrary, he displays a servant's heart. He speaks in kindness to these troubled pilgrims, asking about their well-being, and that of their father. As they bow down their heads and prostrate themselves before him, he speaks to Benjamin, and says, "God be gracious to you, my son."

If there is any doubt as to the grace and mercy of the lord of the land, note how his heart yearns for his brother, leading him to make haste, seeking somewhere to weep in private. The Hebrew says literally, "His mercies were heated up." His heart yearned for his brother. He wept over him. He showed his brothers grace. He showed his mockers mercy. He showed his betrayers kindness. He showed those who had sinned against him compassion. He accepted those who rejected him. He did not treat them as their sins deserved. Here is the heart of grace: it looks upon those who have done wrong, and does not respond in kind. On the contrary, it passionately desires to show mercy.

The height of Joseph's mercy is seen most clearly, however, in the banquet he prepares for them. He makes arrangements in verses 31–34:

> Then he washed his face and came out; and he restrained himself, and said, "Serve the bread."
>
> So they set him a place by himself, and them by themselves, and the Egyptians who ate with him by themselves; because the Egyptians could not eat food with the Hebrews, for that is an abomination to the Egyptians. And they sat before him, the firstborn according to his birthright and the youngest according to his youth; and the men looked in astonishment at one another. Then he took

servings to them from before him, but Benjamin's serving was five times as much as any of theirs. So they drank and were merry with him.

The healing balm of grace has had quite an effect upon the brothers. Benjamin has been singled out, not only by their father Jacob, but now by the lord of the land himself. And how do the brothers respond? There is no jealousy; there is no hatred; in fact, they sit down to drink and are merry! The brothers do not treat Benjamin as they once treated Joseph. The brothers have changed. Their hearts have been softened. The lord of the land unexpectedly treated them with grace; the Lord of providence did not seem to be against them after all. Could there be forgiveness for their sin? Could their guilty consciences at last be silenced?

The healing balm of grace, administered by the lord of the land, who served these pathetic sinners in his own home, at his own table, from his own hand, has brought them from fear and misery to joy and merriment. Through his service in administering the balm of grace, the lord of the land has taken away their fear, their misery, their hunger. Though custom forbids Joseph to eat with them at the same table, his heart of mercy and grace finds a way: Joseph, the lord of the land, serves his sinful brothers! He takes servings to them! This is Joseph's exalted ministry to his brothers! He takes from his own table and gives to them. He himself serves his brothers—those brothers who once sat down by the pit where they had cast Joseph, turning a deaf ear to his cries, eating and drinking amongst themselves. This Joseph, once despised and rejected by his brothers, now serves them from his own abundance!

⤞⊶⊷◆⊶⊷⤟

And here, in the Word of the Lord, the Lord of the Word wants us to see his exalted ministry to us—a ministry of service. He came to us; we did not come to him. He came to us; we rejected him. We rejected him, our elder brother, even putting him to death. Yet he does not treat us as our sins deserve, but instead calls us "brethren." And he serves us—O how he serves us! He serves us in grace! He serves us in mercy! He serves us in abundance! He takes of his own and gives to us! All that he has is ours! Of his fullness we have all received and grace for grace!

We see it at the table of the Lord, where our Beloved stands in our midst and says, "Come to me! Eat of my fullness! Drink of my fullness! Eat, drink, and be satisfied, my beloved! I gave my body to be broken for a complete remission of all your sins! I shed my blood—the blood of the new covenant—for a complete remission of all your sins! All of this is for you! All that I have is yours!"

> What food luxurious loads the board,
> when at his table sits the Lord!
> The wine how rich, the bread how sweet,
> when Jesus deigns the guests to meet![5]

Is your life filled with misery? Is your conscience plagued with guilt and shame? Then come to Jesus, sit down with him at the banqueting table he has prepared for you! Find your joy and your merriment there in Jesus Christ, your blessed Savior. He came to seek and to save that which was lost. Of this he assures us at his table—the one who comes to him, he will in no wise cast out:

> Love bade me welcome: yet my soul drew back,
> Guilty of dust and sin.
> But quick-ey'd Love, observing me grow slack
> From my first entrance in,
> Drew nearer to me, sweetly questioning
> If I lack'd anything.
> A guest, I answer'd, worthy to be here:
> Love said, you shall be he.
> I the unkind, ungrateful? Ah, my dear,
> I cannot look on thee.
> Love took me by the hand, and smiling did reply,
> Who made the eyes but I?
> Truth Lord, but I have marr'd them: let my shame
> Go where it doth deserve.
> And know you not, says Love, who bore the blame?
> My dear, then I will serve.
> You must sit down, says Love, and taste my meat.
> So I did sit and eat.[6]

5. Charles H. Spurgeon, "Amidst Us Our Beloved Stands," cited from the *Trinity Hymnal* (Suwanee, GA: Great Commission Publications, 1990), #427.

6. George Herbert, "Love (III)," in George Herbert, *The Complete English Poems* (New York: Penguin, 1991), 178.

To bring you from misery to joy, from shame to honor, from guilt to innocence, from sin to righteousness: this is the exalted ministry of Jesus Christ to you, his beloved brother, his beloved sister. His exalted ministry to you is not one of wrath, but one of mercy and grace—grace upon grace!

And so the chapter ends. All is well for the brothers: their fear, misery, and emptiness are gone; they drink, they are merry, they are full. Unbeknownst to them, however, greater provisions are still to come; the lord of the land, who has just served them in the abundance of grace, has not yet shown his face. The best is yet to come.

And so it is for you and me. All is well now, our fear, misery, and emptiness are gone; we have supped with our Lord at his table. But greater provisions are still to come; our Lord Jesus Christ, who has just served us in the abundance of grace, has not yet shown his face. For those provisions let us continue to hunger, let us continue to thirst, let us continue to long. In the meantime, let us be satisfied with the goodness of his house, with the blessings of pure, free, undeserved, unmerited grace, and let our misery be gone, our consciences be stilled; Jesus has provided a complete remission for all our sins—this is the exalted ministry of Jesus Christ, Lord and Servant.

4

ROCK OF AGES

Exodus 17:1–7

Julius J. Kim

Introduction

No one has made more of an impact on my preaching ministry than Ed Clowney. In fact, many will recognize that Ed Clowney himself preached on this text in his exemplary book on Christ-centered preaching, *The Unfolding Mystery*.[1] It was this book and his teaching that introduced me to the profound gospel-centered redemptive-historical tradition of preaching that Westminster Seminary has come to epitomize—in large part because of Ed Clowney's influence.[2]

Prior to coming to seminary, my idea of what constituted a "good" sermon was based on three factors: length (the shorter the better),

---

1. Edmund P. Clowney, *The Unfolding Mystery: Discovering Christ in the Old Testament* (Phillipsburg, NJ: P&R, 1988), 109–28.
2. Other influential books by Ed Clowney include *Preaching and Biblical Theology* (Phillipsburg, NJ: Presbyterian & Reformed, 1979) and *Preaching Christ in All of Scripture* (Wheaton, IL: Crossway, 2003).

style (the more entertaining the better), and passion (the more it inspired my pursuit of holiness, the better). The preachers I regularly heard in the immigrant Korean church in which I was raised tended to interpret and preach Scripture without Christ as the central hermeneutical and homiletical focus. Characters like Abraham and Paul were commended as models of sincere faith and loyal obedience—both excellent qualities in honorable Korean youth. On the other hand, men like Adam and Judas were criticized as the antithesis of proper moral behavior. Thus, Scripture became nothing more than a source book for moral lessons on Christian living, whether the examples were good or bad. This was the controlling preaching paradigm I brought with me to seminary.

Surely the pursuit of Christ-like holiness is and should always be an important element of our ministry of preaching. Furthermore, doesn't God himself make ethical demands of his people—whether they are Israel or the church (e.g., Jesus' own teaching found in the Gospels)? What I discovered in my years under the kind of preaching that emphasized moralism without the proper means and motivation, however, led me to an ever-growing sense of despair. Aside from the physical toil of having to awaken at dawn for daily early-morning prayer meetings, the preaching diet I regularly received nurtured within me a fatiguing and frustrating roller-coaster life of self-righteousness (on the days when I was seemingly upright) and self-contempt (on the others when I encountered the frustrating reality of my ever-present sin). All I knew was that my Christian life never seemed to be secure from within or stable from without.

Then I met Edmund Prosper Clowney. In my first year of seminary, one of the books I was encouraged to read was *The Unfolding Mystery*. I could not know then how that little book would trigger a dynamic sequence of events that would culminate not only in the transformation of my preaching paradigm, but also in my teaching of homiletics in the footsteps of my mentor. Simply put, Ed helped me understand how Jesus himself read the Scriptures. Jesus provided the paradigm for interpreting (and preaching) the Scriptures. After his resurrection, Jesus encountered two despondent disciples on the road to Emmaus. Along the journey, Luke records for us the following: "And beginning with Moses and all the Prophets, he interpreted to them in all the Scriptures the things concerning himself" (Luke 24:27). What Ed poignantly related in his book and in his teaching was that this simple yet significant statement contained the crucial paradigm for preaching—since the purpose of all the Scriptures pointed to Jesus Christ, his person and work are the key component for the faithful interpreting and preaching of Scripture. Thus it is no coincidence that another book by Ed is entitled *Preaching Christ in All of Scripture*. In that book Ed wrote about preaching Christ from the Old Testament: "No revealed truth drops by the wayside in the course of God's redemption and revelation. All truths come to their realization in relation to Christ. If, therefore, we can construct a line of symbolism from the event or ceremony to a revealed truth, that truth will lead us to Christ."[3]

In this way, Ed helped me to understand the importance of distinguishing the Law and the gospel. Contrary to the idea that the Law is only for Old Testament believers and the gospel is for New Testaments believers, the Bible presents Law (commands, obligations) and gospel (promises, the work of Christ) in both testaments. Believers in both testaments are under obligation to live according the moral law of God, in action and in heart. The Bible's clear teaching, however, is that no matter how hard we try, we can never live up to the Law's perfect and prohibitive standards. Judgment and death are thus the just consequences. But the gospel declares that the forgiveness of sin and the declaration of righteousness are available to those who put their faith in the One who paid the penalty for sin and upheld the requirements of the moral law, in action and in heart. Jesus Christ has done it all!

Now the ethical demands, for example, can be preached appropriately without provoking self-righteousness or self-contempt because Jesus has fulfilled all the demands. Thus Jesus gives us the means (Holy Spirit) and the motivation (gratitude) for pursuing holiness. Moralistic preaching that omits Christ's person and work fundamentally teaches that we can reach God on our own, without a mediator. And while this is not the intention of most Christian preachers, when we leave Christ out, it is no longer a Christian ser-

3. Clowney, *Preaching Christ*, 32.

mon. As my other preaching professor, Derke Bergsma, used to say, "If a Rabbi can preach your sermon, it isn't a Christian sermon."

This leads me to my sermon. You may be asking, Why submit a sermon on a text that was so superbly preached by Ed Clowney already? The first reason I chose this text is that it was the first sermon I prepared and preached before Ed during seminary. As one of my Homiletics professors, Dr. Clowney taught me how to communicate the glorious Christ-centered truths found in Scripture in a way that was both faithful to the text and relevant to the hearers. This sermon, then, was the first attempt at putting into practice all that I was learning.

Second, I chose this sermon because it demonstrates that two people can preach Christ-centered sermons from the same text but have very different outcomes. This is because of two primary reasons: the sheep and the singer. After I preached this sermon for class, I was given the opportunity to preach it to a congregation in which I was serving as a pastoral intern. I was therefore forced to answer the "So what?" question. That is, what is the relevance of the truths revealed in this portion of Scripture to the unique group of hearers gathered that Sunday morning in Pomona, California? How does the Christ who is revealed in this portion of Scripture also then direct these hearers in their lives? Because of the distinctive history, experiences, and qualities of these hearers, I wrote and delivered a distinctive sermon for a particular group of sheep. In this way, I was fulfilling my pastoral role as a shepherd who knows the cries of his own sheep.

The sermon is also distinctive from the one found in *The Unfolding Mystery* because of the singer. I tell my students that preaching is both a science and an art. It is a science because there are certain skills that must be learned and objectives that must be met in preparing and delivering a sermon that meets specific standards. However, as each man is created by God uniquely so that no other person in the history of mankind is identical to him, each speaker has his own particular experiences, history, and qualities that impact his preaching. In this way, preaching can also be considered an art. So while two singers may sing the same song, what is heard will be very different due to factors such as the unique timbre of voice and phrasing of words. What follows then is a sermon that, while having echoes of Clowney's tone, is uniquely mine because it was sung with my voice.

I would be remiss if I ended this introduction without talking about another way in which Ed influenced my formation as a preacher. In addition to impacting my preaching with this Christ-centered paradigm, he also influenced my life through his Christ-like piety. He modeled for me how important it is not just to preach Christ from all the Scriptures, but also to live in the presence of Christ. In exhorting preachers to seek and practice Christ's presence in their preaching, he wrote, "We do not seek a surge of power in ministering the Word of God. We seek his presence in the act of preaching, as we hold forth the person of Jesus Christ."[4]

As many who knew him personally will attest, Ed was more than a teacher of preaching. At the end of the day, he was a child of God who reveled in the love that his Father had for him in Jesus Christ. He was keenly aware that his relationship to his heavenly Father was based solely on God's unconditional love for him in the person and work of Christ. So he sought to live in and practice the presence of Christ. I believe this was one of the reasons why Ed had such a humble and gracious spirit. Heart and mind filled with gratitude and the presence of Christ, Ed pursued Christ-like piety.

What should be clear by now is that Ed influenced me in a way that surpasses a preaching paradigm and piety. Where his preaching paradigm and his piety led me was to a person—the Lord and Savior Jesus Christ.

The Scripture (Exodus 17:1–7)[5]

All the congregation of the people of Israel moved on from the wilderness of Sin by stages, according to the commandment of the LORD, and camped at Rephidim, but there was no water for the people to drink. Therefore the people quarreled with Moses and said, "Give us water to drink." And Moses said to them, "Why do you quarrel with me? Why do you test the LORD?" But the people thirsted there for water, and the people grumbled against Moses

4. Ibid., 58.
5. Scripture citations in this sermon are from the ESV.

and said, "Why did you bring us up out of Egypt, to kill us and our children and our livestock with thirst?" So Moses cried to the LORD, "What shall I do with this people? They are almost ready to stone me." And the LORD said to Moses, "Pass on before the people, taking with you some of the elders of Israel, and take in your hand the staff with which you struck the Nile, and go. Behold, I will stand before you there on the rock at Horeb, and you shall strike the rock, and water shall come out of it, and the people will drink." And Moses did so, in the sight of the elders of Israel. And he called the name of the placed Massah and Meribah, because of the quarreling of the people of Israel, and because they tested the LORD by saying, "Is the LORD among us or not?"

The Sermon

"Rock of Ages cleft for me, let me hide myself in Thee."[6]

It's funny how specific songs conjure up particular emotions in me. One such song is the hymn "Rock of Ages." Whenever I sing it, at church or at home, my thoughts fly back to my youth, sitting with my grandmother, listening to her sing this hymn as I eagerly ate the after-school snack she had just prepared for me. Later in life, as she lay dying from cancer, we would sing this hymn together, finding strength and assurance from our God the Rock—especially during seasons of life that were anything but stable.

This hymn, however, always confused me. The first lines of the hymn allude back to the images found in Exodus 33. There is the great Moses up on Sinai asking God to show him his glory. Knowing that Moses could not stand his overwhelming glory, God places Moses into a cleft in the rock, turns him around, and then shields him by his hand as the full *shekinah* glory of God passes by. God thus reveals himself to Moses in this awesome way, promising his powerful and protective presence to his people. So naturally I would expect the next lines of the hymn to extol God for his powerful presence in our lives. But how do the next lines go?

"Let the water and the blood, from Thy wounded side which flowed,

Be of sin the double cure; cleanse me from its guilt and power."

6. Augustus M. Toplady, "Rock of Ages, Cleft for Me," 1776.

Why suddenly the imagery of the cross? Is Augustus Toplady seeing something in Exodus 33 that I hadn't seen? How does being in the cleft of the rock lead to the cross? This first verse of this hymn always perplexed me until I read another passage in the book of Exodus—17:1–7. For in Exodus 17 we come face to face with another Rock, the "Rock of Ages."

We read in Psalm 95:6–11:

> Oh come, let us worship and bow down;
>   let us kneel before the LORD, our Maker!
> For he is our God,
>   and we are the people of his pasture,
>   and the sheep of his hand.
> Today, if you hear his voice,
>   do not harden your hearts, as at Meribah,
>   as on the day at Massah in the wilderness,
> when your fathers put me to the test
>   and put me to the proof, though they had seen my work.
> For forty years I loathed that generation
>   and said, "They are a people who go astray in their heart,
>   and they have not known my ways."
> Therefore I swore in my wrath,
>   "They shall not enter my rest."

As the psalmist here describes this important event in the history of the Israelites, he warns his readers not to follow in the hard-heartedness of their forefathers who grumbled their way throughout the wilderness wanderings. The psalmist goes out of his way to mention the names Massah, which means "trial," and Meribah, which means "strife." For this is no ordinary drama in the history of Moses and the people of Israel. He wants his readers to remember back in the Torah to Exodus 17 where the Israelites decided to take God to court.

And as you will soon see, a legal drama unfolds in the desert courtroom of Massah and Meribah. In this story you will see three major legal elements unfold: a charge will be presented; a verdict will be rendered; and a sentence will be executed.

The Charge

Verse 2 sets the scene in this desert courtroom: "Therefore the people quarreled with Moses and said, 'Give us water to drink.'

And Moses said to them, 'Why do you quarrel with me? Why do you test the LORD?'" The plaintiffs enter the courtroom—the people of Israel. Then comes the defendant—Moses, the covenant mediator for God. How can I say this? The people actually bring a legal charge against Moses. The Hebrew word translated "quarrel" (*rib*) has the connotation of litigation or contention. It is used elsewhere in Scripture in legal contexts with the meaning "to bring suit." In the prophets, for example, it is used to express the lawsuit that God brought against Israel because they broke his covenant.

Who exactly is being charged? The charge is brought against the covenant mediator Moses *and* God himself. Moses replies, "Why do you *contend* with me?" and "Why do you *test* the LORD?" God, via Moses, is being accused of abandoning Israel to die of thirst in the desert. So you must picture it in your minds: Here they are in the hot and arid Sinai peninsula. The scorching sun bakes as it penetrates through the thin cloths wrapped around their heads. Hot winds blow sand into the dry cracks on their faces, searing every portion of their skin. And in this parched land we call the Sinai, weary bodies that have been traveling for weeks become easily dehydrated. So the people cry out for water: "Give us water to drink!" And behind this plea is a charge. They bring an accusation with them. This is no ordinary complaint.

What exactly is the charge? In legal language, this is a breach of contract, otherwise known as treason. In this case, it is a failure to uphold a promise, the promise that God would be their God and they would be his people. Given to their great-great-grandfather Abraham, this promise stipulated that God would deliver them from bondage and multiply them as the sands on the seashore. "But now look . . . we're about to die! Are you among us or not?" Furthermore, in verse 4 we read that Moses fears stoning, which was one of the sentences for treason, betrayal, disloyalty.

So instead of leaving the future up to chance, they decide to take matters into their own hands. They cry out, "You've broken your promise . . . we're not sure if we can trust you, we're taking you to court. We want out of this relationship. We want to control our own future. We don't need you anymore. We want a divorce."

But lest we become too harsh with the Israelites, let's stop and think about it. If we're honest with ourselves, I'm sure you've been in situations when you felt like nothing was going right, when it seemed that God had indeed abandoned you. Recently in my own life I struggled with the same emotions that plagued the Israelites. Holding my grief-stricken wife after a miscarriage, unable to utter a single word, I began to question in my heart, "Where are *you*, Lord? Why give us a baby, only to take it away after just eleven weeks? Are you among us or not?" These are real and honest feelings.

The charge has been recorded. The arguments have been given. What's next?

The Verdict

The Lord tells Moses in verse 5: "Pass on before the people, taking with you some of the elders of Israel, and take in your hand the staff with which you struck the Nile, and go."

Two things are significant about this.

First, as Moses walks ahead of the people, everyone knows that the verdict is "guilty." Guilty as charged. How do we know that? Because Moses goes up with his staff. The people recognize the severity of the matter, for they see their leader Moses walking before them with the staff. This was no ordinary walking stick. This was the staff that was used to strike the Nile, turning it into blood. When Moses struck the Nile, it was a strike of judgment. The Nile River turned to blood in judgment of Egypt's gods and Egypt's disobedience. So now we see Moses going up, not as criminal but as judge. The staff will be used once again to bring justice. This staff was distinctive, for it symbolized God's direct power and judgment.

But another important element demonstrates the serious legal context of the setting. With whom does Moses go ahead of the people? In verse 5 we read that Moses is told by God to take along some of the elders of Israel. Why are they necessary? Again, because of the legal context of this situation, they must formally serve as a jury who will help deliberate over this case. The air was probably thick with anticipation. Can you imagine what the Israelites were feeling? "There goes Moses, and he's carrying that . . . that staff! And there go the elders too. . . ." The tension must have been palpable.

It must have felt like that awkward, uncomfortable feeling you get when you know something bad is going to happen.

But who exactly is the guilty party? Is it Moses? After all, they grumbled against Moses. Is it God? They did put the Lord to the test. But has Moses, or in this case God, been unfaithful?

The Israelites had just recently witnessed one of the most incredible events in the history of their people—an event they would pass down from generation to generation. As they were fleeing Pharoah and his soldiers, the Lord miraculously opened up the Red Sea and allowed them to pass through the sea untouched! And as the last Israelite stepped up on the opposite shore, the Lord engulfed the Egyptians with a mighty roar of the waves. There they stood—*hearing* the cries of the soldiers, *seeing* the dead wash up on the shore, *tasting* the victory of the Lord. *Tangibly* the Lord had shown them his great love and protection. There's more. This is not the first time they have been thirsty. The Lord had already healed the bitter water in Exodus 15. Furthermore, he had provided manna and quail in chapter 16.

Time and time again the Lord has been there for them, yet at the first sign of trouble, they doubt. At the first sign of trouble, they sow their seeds of doubt to reap complaint and rejection. Yes, the desert is a hot and arid place; it's an easy place to dry up, not just on the outside but also on the inside. Jeremiah was so right when he said that the heart is deceitful above all things. Who can know it? Our hearts are so prone to wander, to turn away at the first sign of trouble.

It is at this point that the irony of this courtroom drama emerges. As Ed Clowney wrote so poignantly regarding this passage: "Israel had just been shown God's care in the provision of manna for their hunger, yet they did not trust him to give water for their thirst. They failed to see that they, not God, were on trial at Rephidim."[7] Indeed, they are the guilty party who, at the first sign of trouble, has turned its back on God and betrayed the relationship.

The charge, treason. The verdict, guilty. What's next? The sentencing. The punishment for treason is death! But what about the

---

7. Clowney, *Unfolding Mystery*, 122.

fact that they are God's people? What about the promise that he would multiply their descendants? What about the promise that the Messiah would come from them? If he wipes out the Israelites, what then? Did God have another plan? Did he have another nation as "plan B"? Yet justice must be served.

The Sentencing

Here at the Rock of Massah and Meribah is the triumph of God's grace. Moses is commanded by the Lord to raise the rod of judgment in verse 6: "'Behold, I will stand before you there on the rock at Horeb, and you shall strike the rock, and water shall come out of it, and the people will drink.' And Moses did so in the sight of the elders of Israel." God tells his servant to strike the rock with the staff of judgment. But two seemingly insignificant words appear before this command. Two simple prepositions that make all the difference in not only understanding this passage but also finding comfort in God's grace. God says that he will stand there "before" Moses and that he will stand "on" the rock—"before" and "on." These two prepositions are significant.

First, God declares that he will stand "before" Moses. This is an astonishing statement. Throughout Scripture, especially in legal settings, it is man as the guilty offender who must stand "before" God. It is the guilty criminal who stands "before" the righteous judge. Deuteronomy 19:17 says, "then both parties to the dispute shall appear *before* the LORD, *before* the priests and the judges who are in office in those days." But in this amazing trial at Rephidim, God says he will stand "before" them, taking the place of the accused, going "before" them as the criminal, waiting on the judgment block.

Second, what does it mean that God will place himself "on" the rock? While the Hebrew word used here ('*al*) can mean "before" or "beside," in light of the context it is better translated "on" or "upon." Here God stands "on" the rock, symbolically identifying himself with it. And, while we sing our songs in church extolling God as our Rock, our sure foundation, a bedrock that never moves, God is called "rock" elsewhere in Scripture with different connotations:

Deuteronomy 32:15b: "He foresook the God who made him and
scoffed at the Rock of his salvation."

Deuteronomy 32:18: "You were unmindful of the Rock that bore
you, and you forgot the God who gave you
birth."

Psalm 78:35: "They remembered that God was their rock, that
the Most High God their redeemer."

Psalm 95:1: "Oh come, let us sing to the LORD; let us make a joyful noise to the rock of our salvation!"

A common theme that emerges from these verses shows "rock" as
having *salvific* connotations. Yes, we can praise God as a sure foundation that never moves in times of trouble. But here, the Rock has
connotations of a creator, a *savior*, a redeemer. What is God saying
to his fickle and faithless people?

In the midst of their doubt, despair, and defiance, Israel no longer
trusted that God was in control of their lives. At the first sign of
trouble, they turned their back on God, only to reap judgment for
their rebellion and rejection. But in this amazing trial, God is declaring through the use of these simple prepositions that he will take
their judgment. Though entirely innocent, he will sacrifice himself
and be their substitute. For God's promises to continue, he himself
must receive the charge, verdict, and punishment.

So Moses lifts the rod of judgment and strikes the rock on which
God stands and with which he is symbolically identified. What is the
result? As a result of the striking of the rock, water flows out. Not
just any water, but life-sustaining water. Water that not only satisfies
the mouth but enlivens the soul. For the rock at Massah is not just
any old rock, but it is the Rock of Ages. For in the fullness of time,
Paul would write about the Israelites in 1 Corinthians 10:4 that they
"all drank the same spiritual drink. For they drank from the spiritual
Rock that followed them, and the Rock was Christ."

So here the rock at Massah and Meribah is a type of Christ—a
preview of the full drama that will reveal God himself coming in
Jesus for frail and fragile, faithless and defiant people like you and

me, who sometimes struggle, day after day, week after week, with making sense of God's ways when bad things happen. And when bad things happen, God calls us to remember this rock, the Rock of Ages, who was struck for us so that we might drink fully from the great river of life that flows from his throne (Revelation 22:1–2).

When Jesus died on the cross, and the sword was thrust into his side, what poured out? Blood and water (John 19:34). It's no coincidence that there are all these references to water. You see, this is God's message for you, for you who thirst, who go through parched lives, who find yourselves often in desert situations—to look to the cross. For when we look to the cross, we see a Savior who loved us so much that he received the rod of judgment for our rebellion and rejection. We see our Lord who, though innocent, sacrificed himself in our place.

This is our God. God loved us so much that he did not spare his own Son, but gave him up for us all, so that we might never thirst again. Is the Lord among us? He is not only among us—he has *become like us* in the humility and glory of the incarnation, to endure the punishment of the cross as the wages of our sins: the sin of our hardened hearts, the sin of our independence, the sin of our rejection. What kind of love is this? What kind of grace is this? What kind of provision is this?

In a world that threatens to turn our eyes away from the Rock who created us and redeemed us, let us throw off everything that hinders and turn our eyes to the author and finisher of our faith. Let us "turn [our] eyes upon Jesus, look full in his wonderful face; and the things of earth will grow strangely dim in the light of his glory and grace."[8] Amen.

8. Helen H. Lemmel, "Turn Your Eyes upon Jesus," 1922.

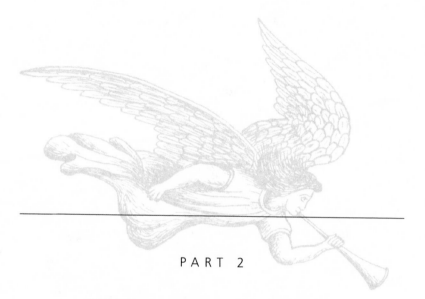

PART 2

THE PROPHETS

5

SURPRISING LOVE

2 Samuel 9

Charles D. Drew

Introduction

I delivered this sermon in the winter of 2005 to my congregation in New York City—a bright and generally driven group of young people. Most of them are either preparing for or are in the hard-working early stages of a professional career (we are situated next to Columbia University).

Like so many in our time these young people express a keen desire to find community. At the same time, they encounter relentless pressure against the disciplines that make for community. Work and study hours are long. Entertainment options abound and can easily eat up discretionary time. Perhaps most problematic, social options abound: there is always another, possibly more interesting, person to meet. In a small town you either marry "Susie" or you don't marry. But in New York, "Susie" may be interesting, but so are "Josie" and "Emily"—and who knows who may come along tomorrow?

The same sort of reality is true regarding church communities. There is always another church community that is more convenient or, in particular ways, more satisfying. So why commit to any one—especially when you leave Manhattan every other weekend—or you will not be in Manhattan too long? Mobility is a huge problem here. People are constantly moving in and out of the city. For the transients it does not make much sense to commit to a church or a small group. And for those who stay behind, it is often too painful to commit to people who may be gone in a year, or it is often too frustrating to schedule weekly gatherings when so many are off the island on business or pleasure so frequently.

For all these reasons, I felt the need to preach from 2 Samuel 9 about the commitments of love that the Bible calls for. But as I sought to do this, I heard the ghost of Ed Clowney whispering in my ear, "If a rabbi could preach your sermon, you will not have taught it as you should." To teach my people to love one another without giving to them the Lord of love is to miss the heart of Scripture's purpose, since Scripture is designed to "make [us] wise for salvation through faith in the Jesus Christ" (2 Tim. 3:15). To call for love without celebrating the Lover is to turn the Bible into a book of moral advice. And to do that is to strip it of its power by urging people to look to themselves rather than the Messiah for the resources they need. So, as I exegeted 2 Samuel 9, I kept asking, "Lord Jesus, where are you here? How does this text help make my dear self-isolating flock—and me—wise for salvation through faith in you?"

My decision to preach 2 Samuel 9 arose out of the commitment I had made to preach through 1 and 2 Samuel—a decision that had its roots in a broader commitment to preach regularly from the Old Testament. That commitment goes back, as far as I can tell, to a lecture I once heard Ed Clowney give, during which he held up a Bible (evidently not his!) and asked us to note which portions of it were well worn and which portions looked like they had only recently come off the press. We didn't even have to open the book to see that the latter one-fifth was much dirtier on the edges than the former four-fifths—shocking when Jesus caused his disciples' hearts to burn as he opened Moses and the Prophets to them on the road to Emmaus. So much fire squandered! So many souls left cold! I don't want this to happen to me or to those I serve.

Anyone who has seen Ed's artwork, or sung his hymns,[1] or read his poetry (he actually wrote one for me, which I prize) knows that a deep love for aesthetics drove him. He did not simply love theology. He loved the beauty of theology—better, the beauty of the God of theology. This I believe is part of why biblical theology was so precious to him. To see the unfolding mystery of Scripture in the revelation of Christ moved him—and it moved me as he spoke of it. It moves me as I study 2 Samuel 9 and note the pattern of Jonathan's love for David—a love that formed the basis of David's unexpected and gracious love for Mephibosheth. For I see in this pattern a reflection of the deeper pattern: the pattern of Christ's love for his Father (Ed taught us that Jesus Christ was not only the Lord of the covenant but also the one true Servant of the covenant)—a love that formed the basis upon which I can and do enjoy the unexpected and gracious love of God. Such patterns weave themselves throughout Scripture and often lead us to discoveries of Christ and his work in places where we might otherwise have found only a hard example to try to emulate.

The Scripture (2 Samuel 9)[2]

And David said, "Is there still anyone left of the house of Saul, that I may show him kindness for Jonathan's sake?" Now there was a servant of the house of Saul whose name was Ziba, and they called him to David. And the king said to him, "Are you Ziba?" And he said, "I am your servant." And the king said, "Is there not still someone of the house of Saul, that I may show the kindness of God to him?" Ziba said to the king, "There is still a son of Jonathan; he is crippled in his feet." The king said to him, "Where is he?" And Ziba said to the king, "He is in the house of Machir the son of Ammiel, at Lo-debar." Then King David sent and brought him from the house

1. For example, "Vast the Immensity, Mirror of Majesty," "We Lift Up as Our Shield God's Name," "Who Shall Ascend the Mountain of the Lord," "In Your Arms, Lord Jesus Christ," "You Came to Us, Dear Jesus," and "O Lord, I Love You, My Shield, My Tower" (Hymns 24, 104, 292, 419, 596, 620, respectively), *Trinity Hymnal* (rev. ed.) (Atlanta: Great Commission Publications, 1990).

2. Unless otherwise identified, Scripture citations in this sermon are from the ESV.

of Machir the son of Ammiel, at Lo-debar. And Mephibosheth the son of Jonathan, son of Saul, came to David and fell on his face and paid homage. And David said, "Mephibosheth!" And he answered, "Behold, I am your servant." And David said to him, "Do not fear, for I will show you kindness for the sake of your father Jonathan, and I will restore to you all the land of Saul your father, and you shall eat at my table always." And he paid homage and said, "What is your servant, that you should show regard for a dead dog such as I?"

Then the king called Ziba, Saul's servant, and said to him, "All that belonged to Saul and to all his house I have given to your master's grandson. And you and your sons and your servants shall till the land for him and shall bring in the produce, that your master's grandson may have bread to eat. But Mephibosheth your master's grandson shall always eat at my table." Now Ziba had fifteen sons and twenty servants. Then Ziba said to the king, "According to all that my Lord the king commands his servant, so will your servant do." So Mephibosheth ate at David's table, like one of the king's sons. And Mephibosheth had a young son, whose name was Mica. And all who lived in Ziba's house became Mephibosheth's servants. So Mephibosheth lived in Jerusalem, for he ate always at the king's table. Now he was lame in both his feet.

The Sermon

Let me begin with two stories. The first is from the film *Out of Africa* starring Robert Redford and Meryl Streep. At one point Ms. Streep's character asks her lover about marriage, to which he responds, "Do you think a piece of paper will make me love you any more?"

We resonate with this statement. Who needs a piece of paper when what we are really looking for is commitment? Love is more important than an outmoded institution! The only (and rather profound) problem with such assertions is that they usually mask a reluctance genuinely to commit.

Here is the second story. It features nineteenth century Princeton theologian Benjamin Warfield and is told by Ralph Davis in his commentary on our passage:

The works of . . . Warfield . . . are still known and read in the evangelical church today. What is not so well-known is the tale of his marriage. Warfield was pursuing studies in Leipzig, Germany, in

1876–77. This time also doubled as his honeymoon with his wife Annie. They were on a walking tour in the Harz Mountains when they were caught in a terrific thunderstorm. The experience was such a shock to Annie that she never fully recovered, becoming more or less an invalid for life. Warfield only left her for seminary duties, but never for more than two hours at a time. His world was almost entirely limited to Princeton and to the care of his wife. For thirty-nine years. One of his students noted that when he saw the Warfields out walking together "the gentleness of his manner was striking proof of the loving care with which he surrounded her." For thirty-nine years.[3]

Introducing this story, Dr. Davis says: "What the world doesn't see is that love that truly loves is willing to bind itself, is willing to promise, willingly and gladly obligates itself, so that the other may stand securely in that love."[4]

We are afraid of this sort of commitment—for numerous reasons. It may be that so many around us (including our own parents) have failed or are failing at it. Why should we expect our lives to be any different? Or it may be that we have little sense of security about our identity. How can *I* promise to be there for you in five or ten years, we wonder, when I don't really know who *I* actually am? How can we promise to be faithful to one another when one, or both, of us may drastically change in five years?

What does it mean to love deeply, and where do we get the power to do it? These are the questions I want to address today as we look at the David and Mephibosheth story.

This story is all about love. To be more precise, it is all about *hesed*, a word that appears three times (in vv. 1, 3, and 7), and whose meaning, rooted as it is in the character of God, is so rich that no single English word can fully do it justice: *steadfast love, lovingkindness, covenant friendship, loyal love,* and *justice* are a few of the ways we translate the term.

Notice three things about *hesed* in David's example: First, it is a priority. Second, it is surprising. Third, it is promise-driven.

---

3. Dale Ralph Davis, *2 Samuel: Out of Every Adversity* (Ross-shire, UK: Christian Focus, 2001), 102.
    4. Ibid., 101.

Top Priority

Consider first the *priority* David gives to *hesed*. David is at last the acknowledged king of Israel, established in Jerusalem after many years of waiting and suffering. And the very first thing he does is to seek for a way to show kindness. No advisor counsels him to seek out Jonathan's son. Nor does that son come to David seeking help. "David asked, 'Is there anyone still left of the house of Saul to whom I can show *hesed* for Jonathan's sake?'" (2 Sam. 9:1, CDD[5]).

The new king sends out an APB: "Find me someone to love for Jonathan's sake! Search the highways and the byways!" And the search goes on until Saul's crippled grandson is found.

David is like this because his God is like this. God called Abraham out of obscurity and made him the father of the nation that would bring healing to the world. God called David out of the fields and made him his people's king. God came to earth in Jesus and, when he came, he went in search of the physically and the morally lame. One of them was Zacchaeus, the lonely and corrupt turncoat tax collector; Jesus invited himself to dinner and changed the man's life from the inside out. Luke declares at the end of the story, "For the Son of Man came to seek and to save what was lost" (Luke 19:10, NIV).

How aggressive is your love for people? Like David, and like David's God, are you on the lookout for people to love? Are you on the lookout to find ways to love people who can't pay you back, people who are weak, people who might even have been your enemies? This is what *hesed* does.

Surprising Generosity

Notice a second thing about *hesed*. It is "over-the-top" generous.

Mephibosheth was the surviving grandson of King Saul—the deeply troubled ruler who had hated David and sought repeatedly to kill him. Mephiboseth's father was Jonathan, David's dearest friend despite Saul's hatred, now dead along with his father. Years before, knowing that David would one day rise to power and replace Saul, Jonathan had asked the following of his friend:

5. Scripture citations marked CDD are Pastor Drew's translations.

But show me unfailing love [*hesed*], like that of the LORD, as long as I live so that I may not be killed, and do not cut off your love [*hesed*, again] from my family—not even when the LORD has cut off every one of David's enemies from the face of the earth. (1 Sam. 20:14–15, CDD)

Hesed means a great deal, as we have already noted. But the particular meaning that Jonathan seems to be giving it here—certainly the meaning that David might have chosen to give it in the light of the wording of Jonathan's request—was pretty narrow and specific. Jonathan is asking, "David, when you come into power, please don't do to me and my family what is customary in regime changes of our day. Please don't kill us."

David refuses the narrow meaning. His application of the promise is expansive. When he finally meets the crippled son of Jonathan this is what we read:

"Don't be afraid," David said to Mephibosheth, "for I will surely show you kindness [literally, "showing kindness, I will show you kindness"—a Hebrew idiom for intensity of expression, something like "Upon my life I guarantee that I will look after you!"] . . . For the sake of your father, Jonathan, I will restore to you all the land that belonged to your grandfather and you will always eat at my table." (2 Sam 9:7, CDD)

Consider what David *might* have done—and been totally within the terms of the promise he had made to Jonathan. He might have provided Mephibosheth with a stipend for life, a few servants to look after him, and a safe place to live. Or, David might simply have left him alone—that is, refrained from killing him. Instead, David restores to him the entire estate of his grandfather (which would have been considerable), provides him with thirty-five servants to work the property (see vv. 9–10), and receives him to his royal table—not just once, but for life.

Imagine you have been waiting for two hours at Broadway and 120th Street to be picked up by a member of the church who has promised to drive you to the church retreat in his fourth-hand 1983 Nissan Sentra. You are about to give up when a Mercedes pulls up.

The driver gets out, hands you the keys and says, "Some guy at the church sent me to give these to you—along with the car itself. Insurance is paid for the life of the car, you have lifetime parking privileges in the garage next to your apartment, and all repairs and maintenance for the life of the car will be taken care of by your personal 24/7 Mercedes mechanic, flown in from Germany just for you. And, of course, when this car dies, there will be another one. Enjoy!"

Over-the-top generosity.

I love the attention to detail in all this provision. For Mephibosheth to have merely been given Saul's land would have been an impossible burden for him to bear—since Mephibosheth did not have the means to care for it. (It would have been a bit like our church being given Madison Square Garden outright, but without the means—financial, technical, and in man power—to manage and maintain it.) The gift would have been an albatross around Mephibosheth's neck. But *hesed* does not love burdensomely. God-like love is not a "giver-centric catharsis," in which I dump a whole bunch of stuff on somebody who is less fortunate so that I can feel good about myself. It is truly "other directed." It is thoughtful as well as generous.

I recently met Dominique and Carla, directors of an international ministry aimed at rescuing women from prostitution and the lifestyle that accompanies it. Dominique told me a story that I won't easily forget. On one occasion early in the ministry's history, they found themselves without money to provide food for the women in the shelter. One of the women, who had a young child, came to Dominique complaining that there was no milk for her child. Dominique said, "I know. We must pray for it." And they did, on the spot, despite the unbelief of the young mother. Within a short period of time there was a knock at the door. The visitor announced that, while praying earlier that day, she had been deeply impressed by the urge to bring milk to the shelter. She had come with so much milk, in fact, that they ended up with the joy of giving substantial quantities of it away.

God does this sort of thing because he is full of *hesed*. And so was David, his anointed king. Full of surprising, and tailor-made, generosity.

There is more. The most astonishing expression of David's "over-the-top" kindness is the place that he gives Mephibosheth at his table. Just so we don't miss this, the narrator tells us about it no fewer than four times! Everything in that cultural setting marked Mephibosheth as David's enemy—a rallying point for Saul loyalists and malcontents. And yet David—who had nearly been murdered at Saul's table—brings Saul's heir to his own. He welcomes him fully and permanently into his household as he would a son. Such treatment not only guarantees Mephibosheth's safety. It exalts him. It confers public honor upon him: lame and without hope, he is elevated to the new king's right hand.

God's love is like this. He is not content simply to see us taken care of—a patron from the other side of town who sends monthly checks to us so that we can buy groceries. He wants us *with him*—he wants to honor us as his children. And what makes this love doubly amazing is that we are *proven* enemies, not just *potential* ones. We may be reconciled to him now, but we have not always been so—and even now we have our moments of rebellion and indifference. What is most astonishing of all about this love is what it cost: our elevation to the king's table cost God much more than some territory that he might have kept for himself. It cost him his life. Listen to Romans 5:6: "You see, at just the right time, when we were still powerless, Christ died for the ungodly. Very rarely will anyone die for a righteous man, though for a good man someone might possibly dare to die. But God demonstrates his own love for us in this: While we were still sinners, Christ died for us" (NIV).

Is our love like this? Is it over-the-top, surprising in its generosity? Does it think through and address the particulars? Is it directed toward the "lame"—those who are in no position to reciprocate? Does it find special joy in conferring honor upon others? Is it fearless, reaching out to those who might turn out to be our enemies? Is it costly?

Promise-Driven Commitment

There is one final feature of David's *hesed* to which I want to call our attention. It is promise-driven. That is, it arises from faithfulness to pledges earlier made.

Remember verse 1 again: "Is anyone still left of the house of Saul to whom I can show *hesed* for Jonathan's sake?"

What drove David's kindness was not human pressure. No one expected it. No one knew about his promise except Jonathan, and Jonathan was dead. What drove David was not a politically embarrassing situation: there was no lame beggar at his gate identifying himself as Jonathan's son and making loud claims upon David's hospitality. What drove the king wasn't a deadline: what sort of deadline applies after twenty years? It wasn't political safety: politics dictated Mephibosheth's death. It wasn't convenience: it would have been easier to ignore the entire situation.

What drove David's kindness was *his word*. He loved Jonathan and had promised Jonathan something. And for David a promise was a promise, no matter how long ago it was made. And now, at last, David was in a position to deliver on the promise. Nothing could remove from his mind the obligation and determination to do so.

David shows us once again what our God is like. God would rather die than break a promise. In fact he did. Having promised in ancient times to rescue us from our bondage to sin and death, he followed through, submitting to the horrors of humiliation, crucifixion, and death in order to bear away our sin and death. God swore to his own hurt (see Ps. 15:4).

Our words tend to be so much cheaper than God's. We make marital promises that at least 50 percent of us formally break, and that all the rest of us break in our adulterous imaginations. We make membership vows glibly: how many of us who are church members can even *remember* the content of the promises we made when we joined? Compromised promises to friends, roommates, professors, students, employees, employers, parents, and children fill our lives. For one reason or another we act as if our words have no weight at all. Perhaps it's because we know we can get away with it—as when I (chronically) arrive home late for an agreed upon dinner because I know my wife will forgive me. Perhaps it's because we have managed to convince ourselves that the obligation of a promise fades with time—as if our word has a half-life, so that what I promised yesterday is only half as weighty as what

I promised five minutes ago, and what I promised the day before yesterday is only a quarter as weighty. Perhaps it is the effect of the Internet: our words *must* be cheap if we can send so many of them to so many people so easily (and, if we choose, anonymously) at such blinding speed.

Perhaps we give our words such little weight because we have allowed ourselves to believe the lie that we ourselves don't matter very much. Why care so much about what you say, a voice whispers incessantly, when you yourself are worthless—short-lived—barely noticed—random?

And God counters: "But you do matter! You can know this because I have said so and my word is an immovable mountain. Can't you see this in the love I gave David for Mephibosheth—a man whom the world had written off, a man who, perhaps, had written himself off?"

Eugene Peterson writes:

> The Mephibosheth story provides stabilizing ballast to counter the stormy emotions that the weather of our times lets loose daily on our ideas and experiences of love. Emotions, of course, are an essential component of love, but not only ecstatic emotions, not exclusively sexually-oriented emotions. There are also emotional dimensions to concern and compassion, to responsibility and kept promises. Loyal-love [*hesed*] is a way of life that works for the good of another, sees behind and beneath whatever society designates a person to be (disabled, inconvenient, a rival, worthless, dysfunctional), and acts to affirm God-created identity.[6]

It is a love that loves to honor—a love that pays a price. It is a love that keeps its word.

So here we have God's standard, displayed movingly in David's first act as king—a love that takes the initiative, a love that is over-the-top generous and costly, a love that is thoughtful and particular, a love that never wanders from promises that have been made. We are to love this way because we are made in God's image and God loves this way.

---

6. Eugene Peterson, *First and Second Samuel* (Louisville: Westminster John Knox, 1999), 175.

The Source of Costly Commitment

The standard is beyond us and forces upon us the question, how do we do this? Where do we find the power to love this way?

Here is the answer. We find the power to love this way in the same place where David found it—in the *hesed* that God bears toward us.

Think about David's experience. David could love Mephibosheth as he did because he had tasted God's faithful and practical love through two stormy decades. Life had not been easy for him (life is not easy!); but he had been fed, sheltered, delivered, loved, and finally vindicated by God. Read through 1 and 2 Samuel for yourself and see. David knew that he was beloved, valued, and safe. He had written, or would one day write, these words from Psalm 27:

> The LORD is my light and my salvation;
>   whom shall I fear?
> The LORD is the stronghold of my life;
>   of whom shall I be afraid? (Ps. 27:1)

Here is the point: When I know that I am safe—eternally and completely safe—in the arms of God; when I know that I have his undying affection and his almighty power to back up that affection; when I know that all his plans for me are good (even the trials, even the time and manner of my death)—*then* I am free to pour out *hesed* upon you. "We love," says 1 John 4:19, "because he first loved us."

But how do I *know* (how do *we* know) that I have God's *hesed*? How do I *know* that I am safe and beloved? How can I be sure, especially when I am so "lame" (if not physically, then spiritually) and such a *dead dog* saint (to use Mephibosheth's language in v. 8)? Because God's *hesed* toward me is not grounded in my performance. It is grounded in the performance of someone else. Don't miss this. It is at the heart of this story, and it is very important to understand.

Why was Mephibosheth so safe with David? Not because of Mephibosheth. Not because of anything that Mephibosheth had done. Not because Mephibosheth had drawn out David's compassion. Not because Mephibosheth had done something to merit David's concern.

Mephibosheth's good fortune had nothing whatsoever to do with Mephibosheth. It had everything to do with Jonathan—which is why David said, "To whom can I show *hesed* for *Jonathan's sake?*

Jonathan had sworn undying loyalty to David. *Jonathan* had surrendered his crown to David. *Jonathan* had loved David unconditionally to the bitter end. Not Mephibosheth, but *Jonathan* was the reason for the pouring out of the king's love upon Mephibosheth.

Now think about yourself. Why are you so safe with God? Why are we? Not because of us. But because of Jesus—the one who gave up his crown to the Father, the one who pledged his love and stayed loyal to his Father to the very end—even though that end meant crucifixion and hell, in obedience to the Father's wishes. Jesus is the one and only man in history who has fully and fairly won the full outpouring of God's abundant lovingkindness. The Father said of him, and of him alone, "This is my beloved Son, with whom I am well pleased . . ." (Matt. 17:5). And the Father has demonstrated his delight by raising him from the dead and declaring him Lord of all.

And now Jesus, our "Jonathan," speaks to his Father on our behalf, saying, "Father, *for my sake*, bring them safely home! Father, *for my sake*, see that they are fully, forever, and in all of the details, abundantly cared for! Father, *for my sake*, bring them to your table to share with me, as joint heirs, in the full bounty of your love and presence! Father, *for my sake*, treat them as you would treat me!"

Jesus desires all to be well between us and the King—not just the King of Jerusalem, but of the universe. And he calls for this *for his sake*—for *Jesus'* sake, not for ours. Not because *our "hesed"* is particularly good—but because *his* is. Dare we doubt that the Father will grant such a request, made in such a name? Dare we think that God will love us any less than he loves his only begotten Son, when that Son has asked him to bind our destiny to his and his to ours?

No! God's *hesed* is ours—now and forever. Jesus' own loyalty seals it to us. Listen to 1 John 3:1–2 and Romans 8:32 and rejoice:

> See what kind of love the Father has given to us, that we should be called children of God; and so we are. . . . Beloved, we are God's

children now, and what we will be has not yet appeared; but we know that when he appears we shall be like him, because we shall see him as he is.

He who did not spare his own Son but gave him up for us all, how will he not also with him graciously give us all things?

Think about the liberty this gives us. People who know such love—people who are certain of it—people like us—can love with abandonment. We can love without fear. We can love without being loved back. We can love with great thoughtfulness. We can love at great cost. We can love "over-the-top." We can swear to our own hurt. We can endure a tough marriage. We can love those who hurt and ignore us. For we are safe and loved ourselves—and nothing, not even death, can take that love away.

6

THORNS AND FIR TREES

Isaiah 55:13

Harvie M. Conn

Introduction

From 1960 to 1972 the late Dr. Harvie M. Conn served as a missionary of the Orthodox Presbyterian Church in South Korea. His ministry in Korea was multifaceted, from theological seminary instruction of future pastors to evangelistic and mercy outreach to prostitutes on the streets of Seoul. In 1972 he and his family returned to the United States—and *into* the city of Philadelphia— in response to a call from Westminster Theological Seminary to teach missions and apologetics, a position that he held until his retirement in 1998. Those who studied under Dr. Conn were profoundly affected by his passion to see Christ's reign of grace advanced in the cities of the world, particularly among the poor and victims of injustice. Dr. Conn had completed Master of Divinity and Master of Theology studies under Edmund Clowney and other Westminster faculty prior to his pastoral and missions service, and his preaching and teaching bore the imprint of his mentors' Christ-centered, redemptive-historical approach to Scripture. In his fore-word as editor of a *Festschrift* for Dr. Clowney, Dr. Conn observed:

> No one who studied under Ed Clowney from 1952 to 1984 ever missed that commitment [to approach practical theology as *theology* controlled by Scripture]. He brought to every course biblical insights shaped by his studies in the history of special revelation. Whether homiletics or Christian education, missions or ecclesiology, each class moved from Genesis to Revelation, drawing together the whole of Scripture with new insights that pointed in a fresh way to Christ and his redemptive purposes. . . . No area of practical theology was untouched. And no discussion began or ended without being touched by the mark of Scripture. That touch was always dox-ological. The doctrines of sovereign grace and God's electing love in Christ are the themes to which Ed consistently returns.[1]

This sermon was preached on September 27, 1992, at Tenth Presbyterian Church in Philadelphia, a historic Presbyterian con-gregation that resisted the twentieth-century trend to move out to "safe" suburbs, resolving instead not only to maintain its location in central Philadelphia but also to make Christ's presence and com-passion known to its neighbors through a variety of outreach and mercy ministries. The occasion was the installation of Dr. Bruce A. McDowell and the Rev. D. Marion Clark as associate pastors of the congregation, and Dr. Conn was invited to preach because he had supervised Dr. McDowell's Doctor of Ministry studies in missiology and because Dr. McDowell's focus of pastoral responsibility was (and still is) to give leadership to Tenth's strong commitment to the global advance of the gospel. To this day Tenth Presbyterian's com-mitment to the city and to the cross-cultural communication of the gospel of Christ resonates with the heartbeat of Dr. Conn's ministry, and Pastors McDowell and Clark continue to provide pastoral lead-ership to this congregation that stands in and for the city.

The editor and the Clowney Legacy Corporation board are grate-ful to be able to include a sermon by Dr. Conn in this collection,

---

1. Harvie M. Conn, ed., *Practical Theology and the Ministry of the Church 1952–1984: Essays in Honor of Edmund P. Clowney* (Phillipsburg, NJ: P&R, 1990), xi.

since his application of insights from biblical theology to issues of missiology and urban ministry exhibit a distinctive and important expression of Christ-centered preaching in the tradition of Edmund P. Clowney. We thank the staff of Tenth Presbyterian Church, who graciously provided the audio recording from which this sermon was transcribed. And special thanks go to Mrs. Beth Conn Neikirk, executrix of her parents' estate, for permission to publish the sermon and for her editorial review of its transcript. Anyone who heard Harvie Conn preach or lecture will appreciate immediately how difficult—actually, impossible—it would be to capture his preaching style on the printed page. It was a unique blend of cheerful, ironic humor (punctuated with chuckles over his own and others' foibles—imagine such a chuckle following every parenthetical comment in this sermon), intense seriousness in confronting the church's complacency and the city's injustices, and joyful wonder and hope in the redemptive power of Jesus the Christ. It would be preferable to hear and see Dr. Conn in person—his big frame, red hair, graying beard, thick glasses, joyful amusement, conscience-searching eyes. But since Christ the King called this faithful herald of the gospel out of his labors on this earth and into the blessed rest of the saints in 1999, "hearing" him on these pages will still challenge your heart and fan to flame your hope in the Redeemer who even now, through the gospel of grace, is uprooting the thorns of this fallen world and planting in their place the evergreens of blessedness and grace. (Editor)

The Scripture (Isaiah 55:10–13)[2]

> As the rain and the snow
>   come down from heaven,
> and do not return to it
>   without watering the earth
> and making it bud and flourish,
>   so that it yields seed for the sower and bread for the eater,
> so is my word that goes out from my mouth:
>   It will not return to me empty,
> but will accomplish what I desire
>   and achieve the purpose for which I sent it.

2. Unless otherwise identified, Scripture citations in this sermon are from the NIV.

You will go out in joy
    and be led forth in peace;
the mountains and hills
    will burst into song before you,
and all the trees of the field
    will clap their hands.
Instead of the thornbush will grow the pine tree,
    and instead of briers the myrtle will grow.
This will be for the LORD's renown,
    for an everlasting sign,
    which will not be destroyed.

The Sermon

I draw your attention particularly to that last verse, and to the line that says "instead of the thornbush will grow the pine tree." This vivid picture is our theme.

We are here to install our two brothers as associate pastors of this church. Now some of you may not really believe this, but becoming a pastor and serving as a pastor in this day is not an easy job. The last time I preached in this church was many years ago now. You may have noticed, some of you have even commented, that my hair is still sort of red, but my beard has changed. (Life has become difficult!) I've also noticed in the intervening years that I'm writing considerably smaller, so I have to hold my notes closer! Being a pastor today is no easy job.

Over the last few weeks I've been reading over two or three different volumes, laying out the kinds of things that a pastor must do today to have a church that grows. There are lots of these books. They're very depressing. As you look through them you begin to get a little concerned. (Your wife usually gets a little desperate!)

"Worshipers," I read in one book, have now become "consumers." Pastoral leaders, I am told in another book, no longer can "control" the church. They must "unleash" it. (Sort of brings up images of the Philadelphia Zoo!) People, I am told, no longer "join" the church; they "buy into" a relationship. (The deacons will be glad to hear about this!) New churches, I'm told in still another book, are no longer known by their doctrine but by their statement of purpose: how will we minister?

The old words, the old buzz words that some of us used to understand, are changing. When we talked about people of "like faith," we were talking about similar doctrine. People of "like practice" referred to similar lifestyle. Well, the new word today is people of "like ministry." That's the new direction.

Even the vocabulary of the ministry is changing. When we came back from Korea in 1972, we had to learn a whole new set of words. Even these words are changing on us now. We talked about the "Me" generation, the "singles." (I used to think about cheese that way.) Now we talk about "dysfunctional families." The other day on television I heard a new one: "granny dumping." Now I've heard there is malpractice insurance for pastors. (Boy, I'm dead in the water!)

Behind all of the changes, of course, is our world. Our world is changing very rapidly. In the world in which I grew up "crack" referred to a break in the mirror. It doesn't anymore. In our cities we have to be afraid of dying from Lipton Soup and Tylenol. In Philadelphia we hear of three-hour-old babies abandoned in supermarkets. The expression "guardian angel" does not call to mind wings from heaven but red berets in the subway. It's a different world.

Into this world, and into this church, we now set apart two men as associate pastors. (We've locked the doors so that at this point they cannot leave. It's too late!) Ahead of them are all kinds of things: long hours, as their spouses can testify, longer nights, administration headaches, too many jobs, too many meetings, too many people, too many demands, too many "too manys." You find yourself asking: is it going to be worth it, after all? Is that "light at the end of the tunnel" the headlight of an on-coming train? Where do we find our perspective?

I think part of our answer comes from this great passage in the book of Isaiah. I think Isaiah answers that question for us in the text that I've laid out for you this morning: "Instead of the thornbush will grow the pine tree. Instead of briars the myrtle will grow."

Now, Isaiah is asking a question, as it were, of Israel in this passage. He's asking, "How does your eschatological garden grow?" You've heard all those spots that come on the local radio station every twenty minutes. The fellow usually ends up making you feel very depressed as he tells you what you are doing wrong with your garden, or alerts you to the latest seeds you should be planting *now* before the first snow comes. (I find that very depressing!) But behind his advice is a good intention, to get you a fairly nice garden.

Isaiah is talking about that, only he's looking at it theologically. He answers this kind of question in what you might call a feature length cartoon style. We read the passage from verses 10 and following, and as you heard that passage perhaps your mind formed a certain picture. You saw the rain coming down, right? In verse 10 the snow from heaven is on its way. (And no snow blowers available!) As you watch Isaiah draw this picture, you also see the earth breaking forth into a new spring. You hear Isaiah describing the seed that's being given to the earth. You hear about bread that is provided to the eater. It's a marvelous picture here. Then you watch as the passage goes on about these mountains and hills; and suddenly they burst into song before you. Now, that would be something to see, sort of a sanctified square dance, if you will. And you watch as these mountains and hills engage in some very undignified, formerly very improper, hand clapping. (These mountains and hills are obviously not Presbyterian!) Then as you see all of this, you see a mighty transformation that climaxes this marvelous picture of Isaiah. You see before you, not thornbushes, but fir trees or junipers. You see not briars or nettles (those awful things that jump at you), but you see myrtles. A magnificent transformation. Useless, offensive plants disappear, and in their place come these noble trees.

In one of the great commentaries on Isaiah, Dr. Edward Young comments that this growth is very rapid growth. On the basis of the Hebrew language (about which I know very little!), Dr. Young concludes that when the writer says "instead of the thornbush *will grow* the pine tree," behind this language is the idea of not just ordinary "come-along-as-it-will" growth but very rapid, accelerated growth. Something very exciting is going on here.

I am sure you know by now that Isaiah here is doing a lot more than drawing a beautiful illustration. Illustrations in Isaiah always have a way of catching you when you are not looking. They have a way of sort of coming up on you and suddenly doing much more than just telling you a neat story you can pass on to the kiddies. These picture stories are imagery that becomes Isaiah's way of talking theology—Isaiah's way, particularly in this passage I submit, of describing the coming day of the Lord.

Throughout the book of Isaiah you will find these same metaphors or pictures appearing again and again. Probably one of the most powerful is very early in the book. In the fifth chapter Isaiah is describing God's people. He describes them as a vineyard that has been planted by the Lord himself. It is a vineyard planted, says Isaiah, to bear grapes. But something has happened, and we are told that this vineyard planted by the Lord is bringing forth wild grapes. So the Lord says that he is going to tear down this vineyard, and something will come up in its place. In verse 6 the message gets very clear: "I will make it a wasteland, neither pruned nor cultivated; and briars and thorns will grow there. I will command the clouds not to rain on it."

Suddenly we are introduced to this picture of briars and thorns. You will notice that some of the very same language is used here that you saw also 55:13. There is no rain to rain on it, Isaiah says. There is no tree of life to maintain it, only briars and thorns. You will overhear that language in Isaiah repeated. You'll hear it, for example, in chapter 7: "And it shall come to pass in that day that every place where there were a thousand vines . . . shall be for briars and thorns" (7:23, ASV). And you will hear it in chapter 10 with these words: "And the light of Israel will be for a fire, and his Holy One for a flame; and it will burn and devour his thorns and his briers in one day" (10:17, ASV). And you will hear it in chapter 32:

> They shall smite upon the breasts for the pleasant fields, for the fruitful vine. Upon the land of my people shall come up thorns and briers; yea, upon all the houses of joy in the joyous city. For the palace shall be forsaken; the populous city shall be deserted; the hill and the watch-tower shall be for dens for ever, a joy of wild asses, a pasture of flocks. (Isa. 32:12–14, ASV)

You can't escape the picture of briars and thorns: God's judgment, God's hand of desolation laid on his people. The picture is that of a wilderness, a wasteland. The mighty cedars of Lebanon have been cut down by the axe of God himself. Isaiah pictures God's people as a field of dead tree stumps. In between the dead tree stumps are all these acres and acres of briars and thorns.

But not forever! In this marvelous fifty-fifth chapter once more the prophet picks up this theme. Now God promises to replant his field. The water of the Spirit is going to be poured out on Israel from on high. He says in chapter 32 that this wilderness that God has made, he will make into a fruitful field. Then he will take this fruitful field and he'll multiply that into a forest—the green revolution of God (32:15). And God is going to do it.

"The desert shall rejoice and blossom as the rose." Do you remember that language? It shall blossom abundantly and will rejoice forever with joy and singing. The glory of Lebanon shall be given unto it. In the wilderness shall waters break out, streams in the desert. This is beautiful, gorgeous language.

Now, what does all of this mean? I think that surely there is a lot more here than simply a description of revival in the church, although I know these texts have been used that way. I want to offer a small suggestion, something for you to sort of chew on. I want to suggest to you that Isaiah here is talking about eschatology; he's talking about the last days. And specifically he's talking about "the day of the Lord." He's talking about the marvelous day when God is going to come, when Immanuel is going to be with us. He's talking about the day, in the language of Isaiah, when the branch is going to bear fruit, when the branch will spring up from the stem of Jesse (11:1). He's talking about that day.

To describe it he uses all kinds of language in the Bible from his own pictures and from earlier books of the Scripture to draw it. You notice in verse 12 he says you will *go out* in joy. That language, "go out"—does that ring any bells? Well, for some of you it should ring an "exodus bell," because this is the language used in Scripture to describe the coming out of the children of Israel from Egypt in the exodus. Now the prophet is talking about a new exodus that God's going to take care of. Once more we're going to go out, only this time it will be in total joy. You notice the other language: You'll *"be led forth"* in peace." Remember that pillar-cloud that you saw in that old Cecil B. DeMille movie? There it was, protecting the children of Israel by day and night, and of course the children of Israel followed the cloud through the wilderness: "You will be led out." It's all here, isn't it?

Once more Isaiah is talking about God coming to start this whole new exodus plan, only in this new exodus there are no obstacles in the way: no Red Sea, no mountains, no hills. Hills can get in the way. Any of you who are climbers and walkers know that hills make hiking harder. "No, not this time," says Isaiah. This time the mountains, mind you, will break out before us. They are going to get out of the way. That is why they are dancing and singing. They are happy to move out of the way, so we can march on through. This ringing cry for joy, no more groaning and travailing in pain for the whole creation. Now, says Isaiah, you can watch the hills and the mountains and the whole creation not just groaning with pain like a woman about to be delivered, but now it is *redemptive joy*. It's the joy of the child delivered at last, because now the Lord has come. It is a beautiful picture.

You find yourself asking as you read it, "When is this marvelous day of growth going to take place? Boy, I am looking forward to springtime, no more thorns and thistles."

Well, hang on there. *Suggestion:* this day of growth that Isaiah predicts *now has started*. It started nineteen hundred years ago. It started with the words of a prophet, rather ill-kempt and not neatly dressed, but with a message, the message of John the Baptist. You've been struck by the kind of agricultural language that John uses when he introduces Jesus. Now that is not simply so that John can identify with all those farmers out there in the audience. That's John the Baptist drawing on prophecies from the Old Testament. That is John the Baptist saying: "Remember these words from Isaiah about thorns and thistles and vines that don't produce? Well," says John the Baptist, "here's the harvester. This great day of harvest has started. The harvester is here. His fan is in his hands to cleanse the threshing floor. He's going to gather the wheat into the garner. This is the agricultural day of God" (see Luke 3:16–17).

Jesus comes as the harvester, doesn't he? He announces his ministry as a ministry of harvest, doesn't he? The harvest is great, says Jesus. He says that this marvelous day of growth has begun, doesn't he? Have you noticed how frequently in the stories of Jesus, which we call the parables, so often these stories revolve around agricultural things? He talks about sowers. He talks about seeds. He talks about things growing so wild and fast that you can throw one seed in the ground and it multiplies two-fold and six-fold and ten-fold. One seed of corn, ten stalks of corn, says Jesus. Over the years and despite all of our urbanization, these are still powerful illustrations, aren't they? But they are more than illustrations. This is Jesus dipping back into Isaiah to all these metaphors. This is Jesus reminding you that this great day when God's going to grow something new has started. It has started because the Grower is here.

In fact the Grower has become the seed himself, hasn't he? Isaiah talked about this day of fir trees instead of thorns, myrtle trees instead of briars. Jesus says, don't wait any longer. You are looking at mountains that might move around in joy. Remember the language of Jesus? If your faith is centered in me as Messiah, look out, because mountains will move with joy into the sea. And he reflects on this great prophecy in Isaiah 55. Remember him talking about the grain of wheat? He talks about the grain of wheat being cast into the earth to die. He says, "If it dies, it produces many seeds" (John 12:24). He's thinking about his own death, isn't he? He's thinking about Calvary. He's thinking about the spilling of that grain of wheat into the earth, and then from that grain of wheat will come life and an abundant harvest. God's kingdom is growing: first the blade, then the ear, then the full corn in the ear. We can rejoice because the harvest is here. God has come to do something marvelous and wonderful in our midst.

We are setting apart this morning two associate pastors who are part of that great harvest planting of the Lord. What a marvelous time to be a pastor!

In the mid-1960s a small group of people, meeting just a few blocks north of here, began worship services. They had no money, pennies amongst them. They started in a beauty parlor in Northwest Philadelphia. There was a preacher among them, without a college degree—as I remember not even a high school degree. It was a church without a building and without a budget. But they started in the mid-1960s, not the greatest time to start a church. Three times, at least, that church moved during the next few years. Finally, just a few years ago, they were able to buy abandoned property, property that some of us remember as the old Connie Mack baseball stadium. On that property they put up their first building. It wasn't a church; it was a twenty-one-store shopping mall, one of the first shopping malls built in the city, and in one of the highest crime rate areas of Philadelphia. Shopping centers had moved out of that neighborhood because of the tremendous fears about shoplifting. An associate pastor talked to me a year ago and said, "We haven't had any shoplifting." The name of the place: Hope Plaza.

Then came the church. In fact, I think just about three weeks ago, their new church building was dedicated right on that plaza on Lehigh Avenue. There they are. The membership in the mid-1960s was maybe six or seven. Now it's ten thousand and growing. They have a Bible institute and a staff of over forty people doing evangelistic work, ministering on the streets. They have a crisis counseling center that operates twenty-four hours a day on the phone. They have plans for a retirement home to go up in that same area, and a Christian school. Deliverance Evangelistic Church.

Exciting, isn't it? Why does it grow? Associate Pastor Wes Pinnock was talking to me a while back. I asked him this question. "Well," he said, "we've never forgotten our original purpose: to win the lost for Christ." *Fir trees instead of thorns.*

Bronx, New York: not the first place you'd go to look for fir trees. In the Fordham area of the Bronx, in the last twenty years, the population has dropped by 20 percent. Right now as you look across the expanse of the Bronx, you are going to see large boarded up apartment buildings, abandoned lots, trash everywhere you turn. Forty-four percent now live below the poverty line in that part of the Bronx. Forty-two percent are unemployed. Abandoned houses, problems . . . nothing can grow here. In the center of it all is a church, not the biggest one in the world. It's called the Love Gospel Assembly. (You can tell by the title it can't be Presbyterian!) It is a multi-ethnic church now, with over three hundred members. It began only about fifteen years ago. The membership is drawn from the neighborhood, so there are former drug addicts, former prostitutes, homeless, alcoholics, and homosexuals. AIDS patients are targeted specifically.

The church ministries are as wide as you want; and yet, interestingly enough, they are limited by their general proximity to the church building. The philosophy of this church is that they want *a walking church*, not a driving church. So the church focuses tightly on its narrow community and presents the gospel. Door-to-door evangelism, street meetings on a weekly basis. They have what they call a "love kitchen," which is a lunch program that feeds six hundred people a day. They have care services staffed by volunteer counselors. They have a full-time lawyer. They have a coffee house ministry the last Saturday of every month. *Fir trees instead of thorns.*

⋗⋅⊷⊶∘⊷⊷⋅⋜

What can an associate pastor look forward to? I almost hate to say it. Well, in another sense, I don't. You can look forward to leading Muslims to Christ. You can look forward to sudden calls at night, a new believer that has just been involved in a critical car crash. Structuring a new evangelistic program for the church, Bible studies with questions you can't answer, and maybe one businesswoman who always seems to ask them. Then eight weeks after the start of the program she'll come to Christ. *Fir trees instead of thorns.*

I was at my presbytery meeting yesterday. I don't usually go to presbytery meetings to get a blessing (only a fellow presbyter will understand that comment!). These are business meetings, so you take a heavy book with you. But an amazing thing happened yesterday. It happened during the coffee break. (All the blessings happen during coffee break time!) And this one came from an old friend of mine. He used to visit our home in Korea where he was a GI. We talked to one another about the gospel. He came back to the United States, and now there he is in this neighborhood. He does not look like the most reputable person in the world. His beard goes down to here, and his hair is almost as long. He wore coveralls. I think I was the only one sitting next to him in the presbytery. We started talking. He is now ministering in Prison Fellowship. He began to ask me to pray for people. He began throwing cards to me and giving me names and information faster than I could compute it. He is doing Bible studies in prison in the area of New Jersey. He started talking about all of the people in his study, excited about how people are listening to the Lord. He said, "You know, in prison when you get serious about the gospel, it's really serious. You don't get many people who give you false professions in prison. Your commitment shows too quickly, and in too realistic a way."

He said, "I was so surprised. I had a marvelous Bible study lately with so many people really serious about the gospel. Generally, I don't ask what their backgrounds are and why they got there. Recently someone told me, and I wished I hadn't asked. There's a woman who's been in my Bible study. We'll call her Ellen. She's been in the news recently in northern New Jersey, a mass murderer." There are three members in his Bible study who have committed between them at least twelve murders. Then there is a quiet mild-mannered fellow who has only shot one person. And he said, "It's amazing to me. They just eat up the Bible. They are so desperate to hear that there is good news. And that the good news is Jesus." *Fir trees instead of thorns.*

And associate pastors who are here to share with us those great, grand pieces of good news. Jesus plants *fir trees instead of thorns*.

Let's pray: Lord, touch the lives of your people with your Word. Thank you for the great hope of the gospel. We do not dredge away our lives in an empty wilderness, but the Spirit has been poured out on dry and thirsty ground, and streams flow through the desert, and fir trees grow because Jesus has come. Thank you for those who minister in our midst, these two who today we especially set apart for that ministry. We express our love for them to you, Father, and we rejoice in that exhibition of your love for them in this occasion. Bless their ministry among us, and bless our ministry together in the power of the Spirit. In Jesus' name. Amen.

7

NO CONDEMNATION

Zechariah 3

Iain M. Duguid

Introduction

I can still remember where I was when I heard my first Ed Clowney sermon. I was sitting in the basement of the library at Westminster Seminary in Philadelphia, listening through headphones to an ancient cassette tape that had been assigned to us for one of our preaching courses, "Jesus Christ and the Lostness of Man."[1] This sermon, originally preached at InterVarsity's Urbana conference in 1973, gripped me from its opening, in which Ed recast an ancient Egyptian love song in his own words as if it were written to a contemporary audience. In what followed, he took one of the oldest passages of Scripture, Psalm 90, and brought its message to bear on an audience primarily made up of college students in a way that focused their eyes powerfully on the gospel. I was immediately

---

1. Edmund Clowney, "Jesus Christ and the Lostness of Man," in *Preaching Christ in All of Scripture* (Wheaton, IL: Crossway, 2003), 151–64.

hooked on the idea of preaching Christ from the Old Testament: it has been my passion ever since.

That sermon by Ed Clowney, which is a classic example of his style, is inimitable in many ways. Preachers cannot be cloned, and it would be a mistake to try to imitate the style of others. Ed had an astonishing mastery of ancient and contemporary literature and philosophy; in that sermon, in addition to the Egyptian text, he quotes Samuel Beckett and Albert Camus, Socrates and Michelangelo, first-century businessmen and twentieth-century Freudian philosophers. Yet he was able to bring together all of these diverse sources in a way that won him respect from highly educated unbelievers, while at the same time delivering his message in a style that was simple enough for ordinary people to understand clearly his message. I cannot match his erudition, but can still aspire to find ways of using contemporary culture to illustrate eternal truths.

On the other hand, his focus on the gospel, which gave his sermons an essentially doxological flavor, is something that has deeply impacted my preaching style. Ed always left people "lost in wonder, love and praise" for Christ at the end of his messages, and this is a goal I strive toward in every sermon. This constant focus on the gospel is not merely an evangelistic strategy to reach unbelievers. By warming our hearts and stirring our devotion to Christ, it is also the means by which believers are equipped best to fulfill our chief purpose as human beings, glorifying God and enjoying him forever. In this way, the same message speaks both to believers and unbelievers, and it is my assumption and prayer that both groups are present every time I preach.

Nor will preaching that focuses constantly on the gospel lead to antinomianism and careless behavior on the part of believers; on the contrary, if my heart is genuinely filled with the message of Jesus Christ crucified for my sins and raised for my justification, how can I lightly continue in my sins? How can I pretend that my pride is not important, if it necessitated no less a remedy than the death of the Son of God? How can I easily contemplate giving myself over to lust, or gossip, or coveting, if Christ bore the Father's curse for these sins of mine? Equally, a focus on the gospel fills my heart with hope and compassion for the lost. They are no worse sinners than

I: they are merely those who have not yet had their eyes opened by God to behold the beauty of his grace. No one is sunk so low as to be beyond the reach of such good news. No sinner is too lost to be rescued by such a great Savior!

One distinctive aspect of this sermon as an example of Christ-centered preaching is the fact that the central point of *comparison* is a *contrast* between Joshua and Christ—the removal of Joshua's filthy garments and his reclothing in pure festival garb is made possible by a matching reverse journey on the part of Christ. This contrast illustrates the doctrine of double imputation (my sin laid on Christ and his righteousness credited to me), which is as clearly taught in Zechariah 3 as in any text in the Scriptures. Sometimes Christ-centered preaching is too eager to find *parallels* between Christ and the Old Testament character or event, an approach which can lead to forced points of comparison between, say, Christ and Samson, when the real point of contact between the Old Testament text and the gospel is in the way in which Christ is *unlike* his predecessor.[2]

Normally, I preach consecutively through books, in order to communicate biblical truth in biblical proportions, and to avoid the classic trap of preaching my own personal hobby horses. In this way, God's people gain a mastery of entire biblical books, not merely selected texts without contexts. This sermon from Zechariah was an exception. I was working on Zechariah for a commentary aimed at pastors, but I had no particular thought at the time of preaching it immediately. However, the vision of the gospel that the prophet saw in Zechariah 3 gripped me with such power that as I studied it I literally wept over my keyboard. Unlike many of my sermons, which take a great deal of effort and persistence, this one virtually wrote itself, and I knew I had to find a context in which to preach it.

The sermon was originally preached in 1999 at Grace Church in Rancho Bernardo, California, part of the Sovereign Grace network, to a suburban congregation made up of about three hundred people from many different backgrounds and ages. I have since preached it again on several other occasions in a variety of differing countries

2. On how to draw appropriate lines between Old Testament events and characters and Christ, see the helpful discussion in Sidney Greidanus, *Preaching Christ from the Old Testament: A Contemporary Hermeneutical Method* (Grand Rapids, MI: Eerdmans, 1999), 234–77.

and cultural contexts. Some men are resolved never to preach the same sermon twice. However, I have found that in general, when I re-preach a sermon, I cover the passage in a more balanced way, and am able to focus my attention on finding the best illustrations and applications, since the exegetical homework is already in place. I am, however, careful to take the advice of Dr. Martyn Lloyd-Jones to keep careful records of where and when I have preached it, so that I don't accidentally preach it again in the same church!

The Scripture (Zechariah 3)[3]

> Then he showed me Joshua the high priest standing before the angel of the LORD, and Satan standing at his right hand to accuse him. And the LORD said to Satan, "The LORD rebuke you, O Satan! The LORD who has chosen Jerusalem rebuke you! Is not this a brand plucked from the fire?" Now Joshua was standing before the angel, clothed with filthy garments. And the angel said to those who were standing before him, "Remove the filthy garments from him." And to him he said, "Behold, I have taken your iniquity away from you, and I will clothe you with pure vestments." And I said, "Let them put a clean turban on his head." So they put a clean turban on his head and clothed him with garments. And the angel of the LORD was standing by.
>
> And the angel of the LORD solemnly assured Joshua, "Thus says the LORD of hosts: If you will walk in my ways and keep my charge, then you shall rule my house and have charge of my courts, and I will give you the right of access among those who are standing here. Hear now, O Joshua the high priest, you and your friends who sit before you, for they are men who are a sign: behold, I will bring my servant the Branch. For behold, on the stone that I have set before Joshua, on a single stone with seven eyes, I will engrave its inscription, declares the LORD of hosts, and I will remove the iniquity of this land in a single day. In that day, declares the LORD of hosts, every one of you will invite his neighbor to come under his vine and under his fig tree.

The Sermon

We live in an age that loves courtroom dramas. Whether it is the various television depictions of people bringing their cases before a

---

3. Unless otherwise identified, Scripture citations in this sermon are from the ESV.

real-life judge, or the fictional renditions of *Law and Order* or movies like *Legally Blonde*, there is something in all of us that resonates to a great courtroom drama. We love the stylized combat that leads up to the decisive verdict of "guilty" or "not guilty." We cheer as the villains are condemned and the innocent declared free to go. We thrill to the cut and thrust of the lawyer's debate—"Objection . . . overruled." It brings us all of the thrill of sports without the physical contact.

But courtroom dramas are only enjoyable as a spectator sport. It is not nearly so much fun if you, or someone that you dearly love, is the one who is there on trial. Then the cut and thrust takes on a whole new dimension as you hope with every fiber of your being to hear the crucial words, "not guilty." You long for the ordeal to be over, to be vindicated and set free from the whole nightmare, so that you can set about getting on with your life and trying to forget it as best you can.

According to the Scriptures, all human beings have a forthcoming courtroom date with God (Heb. 9:27). Christians of past generations understood that reality well. As a young monk searching for salvation, Martin Luther was overwhelmed by the fear of standing before a righteous God as his judge. Similarly, in his youth, Charles Wesley dreaded coming into the presence of a holy God. It was only after these men understood the doctrine of justification by faith through the righteousness of Christ alone that they were permanently freed from that fear, and could declare with boldness, "No condemnation now I dread."

Many people in the age in which we live, even among those who go to church regularly, would have to confess themselves to be complete strangers to the experience that Luther and Wesley describe. They have never feared God's condemnation. The slogan on their bumper stickers and their clothes says it all: "No fear." When you talk to them about God, they will jokingly make reference to "the Man upstairs," our cosmic chum. Their God is far too much of a gentleman to condemn anyone to hell, they will tell you. You do your best, and he'll do the rest. What is there to fear?

This was not the attitude that Zechariah's hearers would have shared. They knew that they served a high and holy God, a God who is of purer eyes than to look upon evil. The holiness of God had been made radically clear to them because they had only just emerged from the holocaust of the Judean exile, a period in which the wrath of God had been poured out upon his people because of their sin. In 586 BC, the temple had been destroyed by Nebuchadnezzar, the city of Jerusalem had been burned, and their king had been captured and taken to Babylon (2 Kings 25). Everything that was sacred had been desecrated and ruined because of the sins of God's people. Now, seventy years on, a small remnant had returned to the Promised Land and the question that faced them was, could things ever be like they were before? Having experienced for themselves the reality of living under God's condemnation, they desperately wanted to hear the declaration of "no condemnation." They knew that, when you come before a holy God, the correct slogan is not "no fear," but "be afraid, be very afraid."

For a community so desperately fearful of God's condemnation, the opening portion of Zechariah's vision was not very encouraging. They were afraid that their sins would separate them from a holy God, and the vision seemed to confirm their worst fears. The prophet Zechariah saw a vision concerning Joshua, the high priest of the day, whose task it was to stand in the Holy of Holies on the Day of Atonement every year as an intermediary between the people and God. Yet in the vision that Zechariah saw, Joshua was dressed in filthy clothing that would have automatically disqualified him for the task (Zech. 3:3). Actually, the situation is far worse than the English translations make it appear. It is not as if he merely became dirty while working on a project in the garden. The Hebrew word literally means that his clothes were soiled with excrement— something that is not merely dirty, or even disgusting, but intrinsically defiling. He is self-evidently ceremonially unclean, yet he finds himself standing before the angel of the Lord, the one who speaks for God. He is in the presence of the God whose eyes are too pure to look upon sin (Hab. 1:13). This is not simply a problem for Joshua personally. Since he is the people's intermediary with God, if *he* is unfit to be in the presence of God, then the whole sacrificial system is compromised, and all hope for the people of being made right with God is gone.

Nor can Joshua simply turn and slink away in the hope that his absence won't be noticed. For this vision is a courtroom scene in which the angel of the Lord is there as judge, and the Accuser (literally, "Satan") is also present. Although this enemy of God's people has been active from earliest times in the garden of Eden (Gen. 3:1), Satan's identity as the Accuser became more prominent as Old Testament history unfolded. The Babylonian authorities and their Persian successors employed a well-developed spying system, known as "the eyes of the king." Unseen informers reported regularly to the king on various activities of his subjects, leading to punishment for those alleged transgressions. That's the role that Satan delights to adopt, seeking to bring charges against God's people. His very name indicates his activity here: he is present to accuse (*śāṭan*) Joshua, that is, to present evidence before the heavenly court that he thinks should lead to Joshua's condemnation.

This case will not demand great prosecutorial skill from Satan, either. Dressed as Joshua is, it's an open-and-shut case, a slam-dunk conviction. Not even the most highly-paid defense attorney could get him off on this charge. However, this is not a normal courtroom, and this is no conventional case. Before Satan is even allowed to present his evidence, his case is immediately ruled out of order, inadmissible. As Satan is waiting to present his charges, the presiding authority responds: May the Lord rebuke you, Accuser! May the Lord who has chosen Jerusalem rebuke you (see Zech. 3:2)!

It is important to note the significance of this ruling. For years, I read this passage and even preached it, but missed the basic point. The Lord does not merely examine Satan's case and find it wanting because there isn't enough evidence or because the evidence is somehow flawed. Not at all! Rather, he rules any *possible* evidence inadmissible. No charge whatever can be brought in against Joshua. Why not? It is because the Lord has chosen Jerusalem. The Lord's choice of Jerusalem and Joshua's position as one who has been rescued from the fire—brought safely from the holocaust of the exile—mean that he is free from any possible condemnation. He is not merely found "not guilty," he is judicially declared immune from prosecution. In spite of his filthy clothes, it is impossible for him to be condemned by God and cast off.

But God does not simply judicially rule any condemnation for Joshua out of order. He also acts subsequently to cleanse Joshua from his iniquity (Zech. 3:4). What the fire of God's wrath in the form of the exile could never accomplish, God achieves by his grace. He first commands his servants, "Take away the excrement-soiled clothes," which removes Joshua's sin and shame. Then he commands that Joshua be clothed in festival clothes, garments suitable to stand in the presence of the King of kings. In a context where filthy garments represent iniquity, these festival clothes can only represent an altogether new righteousness that accompanies Joshua's new status. This righteousness is not something that is earned or produced within Joshua. It is freely given to him *from the outside*, imputed to him.

Finally, the prophet himself breaks in and requests the completion of this act of reclothing by a clean turban being placed on Joshua's head (Zech. 3:5). This turban is not distinctively priestly clothing; rather, it has overtones of glory and even royalty (Isa. 3:23; 62:3). This is literally the "crowning" moment of the whole ceremony: Joshua is now completely reclothed in ceremonially pure, festival garments in the presence of the angel of the Lord as a sign of God's acceptance of him, and in him, of the people he represented.

Joshua's new clothes are not a signal for him to sit back and bask in his new-found glory, though. When the prophet Isaiah's lips were cleansed by a hot coal from the altar in Isaiah 6, he was given a message for those newly-cleansed lips to declare. So too here, Joshua is first cleansed and then immediately charged with a task and granted a promise. His task is given in verse 7: "to walk in my ways, keep my charge, judge my house and guard my courts."[4] The first two of these requirements—walking in the Lord's ways and keeping his charge—are very general ways of describing faithful behavior within a covenant context, while the second pair specifically identifies what that behavior requires of a faithful priest. Joshua is to judge God's

---

4. Iain Duguid's translation. In Hebrew conditional clauses, it is not always clear where the protasis ends and the apodosis begins. Does the "then" clause begin after "if you keep my charge" (with most English translations) or after "if you guard my courts" (with many commentators)? I have chosen the latter interpretation, since *wᵉgam* does not normally begin the apodosis of a conditional clause (see David L. Petersen, *Haggai, Zechariah 1–8* [Old Testament Library; Philadelphia: Westminster, 1984], 203; Wolter H. Rose, *Zemah and Zerubbabel: Messianic Expectations in the Early Postexilic Period* [Sheffield: Sheffield Academic Press, 2000], 69).

house and guard his courts, that is, to ensure that the worship in the temple is pure and undefiled by idolatry. Along with this charge comes a promise of access among those who stand before the Lord: "I will give you the right of access among those who are standing here." Joshua is not in this on his own; he can take his concerns to the Lord and expect to be heard, and he can also expect to receive guidance and direction from the throne room of God. The staircase to heaven that Jacob saw at Bethel, with angels ascending and descending between God and man, is once again open for traffic (see Gen. 28:12). The Lord will not be silent or distant toward his people any longer.

Even this remarkable promise of divine attentiveness, though, is merely a shadow of things to come. For Joshua and his associates, the whole priestly class, were men of portent: they were a sign of things to come (Zech. 3:8). The fact that they even existed after the holocaust of the exile was a sign of God's blessing, a blessing that had far more to give than the people had yet experienced. Now they had experienced the first fruits of that favor in the return from exile, but the future held far more. In the days to come, God promised, his servant the Branch would come (3:8). This messianic king would bring about the complete and instantaneous removal of the iniquity of this land (3:9). In other words, what had already happened for Joshua in visionary form would one day happen for all of God's people. When that happened, the complete blessing of the restored covenant relationship between God and man would be experienced, described in the classic symbol of each man inviting his neighbor under his vine and under his fig tree.

In the meantime, Joshua's attention was directed to an engraved stone (v. 9). This stone was most probably part of the high priest's clothing, a gemstone with seven facets ("eyes"), which was located on the turban and inscribed with an inscription. Aaron's turban had just such an ornament, engraved with the words "Holy to the Lord," which enabled him to bear the iniquity of the people into the tabernacle before the Lord so that it could be atoned for (Ex. 28:36). In the same way, the Lord had prepared and engraved a new stone for Joshua, marking his commitment to act to remove the iniquity of the land definitively, once and for all.

At this point, some of you are perhaps wondering, *what has all this to do with me? I'm sure that it was very interesting and encouraging for Zechariah's first hearers to know these things, but what can I learn from this vision?*

First, in order to understand the import of this vision you need to know that before a holy God, you too stand condemned by nature. This is the basic fact of life that Zechariah's first hearers took for granted, but our culture struggles to grasp. We are so used to hearing people say, "I'm OK, you're OK," that it comes as a terrible shock to have someone say to us that we're not OK. My wife was once talking to a lady at the gym who told her that she loved their church because the message was always upbeat there. People in her church were all so much in love with Jesus that they didn't need to talk about sin anymore. My wife responded that it is precisely because of the sin that fills her heart that she loves Jesus so much. Amen to that thought! Why would I need such a great Savior, if I weren't such a great sinner?

That concept is extremely countercultural in our society, however. We live among a people who don't think of themselves as standing unclean by nature before a holy God. They think of themselves as basically clean people, with perhaps a small spot here or there that could use a little touch up. They think that they need a little dab with a lint brush, not a total transformation or a complete reclothing. Why would God condemn me forever for a few little mistakes that are hardly worth noticing, let alone calling "sin"? Sin is such a negative word.

Sin is indeed a dreadfully negative word, but it is the word that the Bible chooses to use to describe our natural state. It is not merely a word to be applied to especially bad people, either. According to Romans 3:23, "All have sinned and fall short of the glory of God." Paul is there summing up his argument earlier in the chapter: "None is righteous, no, not one; no one understands; no one seeks for God. All have turned aside; together they have become worthless; no one does good, not even one" (Rom. 3:10–12, quoting Psalm 14). Or, as he tells the Ephesians, "You were dead in the trespasses and sins in which you once walked, following the course of this world, following the prince of the power of the air, the spirit that is now at work in the sons of disobedience—among whom we all once lived in the passions of our flesh, carrying out the desires of the body and the mind, and were by nature children of wrath, like the rest of mankind" (Eph. 2:1–3). We are all by nature sinners, filthy before God.

What makes it worse is the fact that this is true not just of our worst deeds. We are sinners not merely if we sleep around and curse our neighbors and steal from stores, but also when we help little old ladies across the road and give generously to worthy charities. By nature, we do these good things to our own glory and not God's— which is the essence of sin. We do good deeds because others will respect us for them, rather than as an offering of praise to God. We may even do good deeds not so that others will respect us but so that we can respect ourselves. We are inveterately "curved in on" ourselves, which is the heartbeat of sin. I myself can preach an orthodox biblical sermon and still be sinning, because I have one eye on what people are thinking of me, rather than having my whole attention fixed on God.

The true depth of our depravity is thus exposed by the fact that we can be as defiled by our keeping of the Ten Commandments as we are by our breaking of them. As the prophet Isaiah reminds us, our very *righteousness* is as unclean as rags stained with menstrual blood in God's sight (Isa. 64:6). Nor is it any comfort to be reminded that our God looks on the heart, not merely on our outward behavior. If our true heart motives were to be revealed—as one day they will be—then every single action we have ever done would be found to be utterly ruined by our mixed motivations. Like the high priest Joshua, we are all dressed in totally defiled clothes, even as we prepare for our courtroom date with God.

That is the bad news of the passage. However, you have to get your mind around the bad news of the passage, or you won't understand the goodness and beauty of the good news that the passage brings us. For the good news of the passage is that those whom God has chosen will be accepted and granted access into his presence. If, like most of our society, you haven't seen yourself as radically condemned before a holy God, this is no surprise. "Of course, God will accept me," you say. "Why ever wouldn't he, since I'm such a wonderful person?" In fact, the real question for most people is whether I'm willing to accept God: "I'm interviewing right now for the position of 'Deity in My Life.' Let me see if this God of yours measures up to my expectations and gives me the blessings that I seek out of life. If he does, then perhaps I'll accept him into my heart. If not, I'll go and find another deity who does."

For the Bible, given the reality of the first observation—that we are radically defiled—the whole process is the other way around. The question is not, will I accept this God into my life? but, will he accept me into his life? Can someone like me, given what I have done and thought against him, still be included in his people? That's why this chapter is such radically good news: it tells you, "Yes, you can." You too can be received into the presence of a holy God, no matter how filthy you are. No matter what you have done, where you have been, what you have thought and said against God, there is still a way into his presence.

But how can this be? How can God be both just and the justifier of the ungodly, as Paul puts it in Romans 3:26? Is God double-minded, someone who talks tough on sin, but inside is just a big soft teddy bear? How can he be both the holy God, who is of purer eyes than to look upon iniquity, and also the gracious God who takes defiled sinners and brings them safely into his presence? That's where this passage in Zechariah gives us a breathtaking insight into the mechanism of our salvation.

How does God deal with the reality of your sinful state? How does he address Satan's charges against you—charges that are by no means trumped up? God judicially rules those charges out of order because in Christ you have been chosen and brought through the fire. Remember, Satan was ejected from the court in Zechariah's vision because God had chosen Jerusalem as his dwelling place to be in the midst of his people, and he had rescued Joshua from the fire of the exile in order to bring about that reality. In the exile, God had judged his people for their sin; as a result, they couldn't be cast off twice for that defilement. But Joshua and his generation were merely signs of the reality to come. They were living proof that God would not abandon his plan to save his people simply because of their great sin: Israel's story could not and would not end with the exile. The reality to which they pointed forward comes with the arrival of "my servant the Branch," the Messiah.

How does God address Satan's charges against you and me and the reality of our sinful state? He declares the charges against you out of order because they have already been borne for you by Jesus. As a result, they cannot be brought against you any longer. There cannot be any condemnation for those for whom Christ died!

As God's chosen one, the one in whom God truly had come to dwell in the midst of his people, Jesus is the one in whom God rescues us from the fire of his judgment. What is more, he does so by entering the fire of judgment himself. In fact, everything that the high priest Joshua received in the vision became a reality by Jesus making the *opposite* move:

- *Joshua* was clothed in festival garments. *Jesus* had the clothing stripped from his back and divided among his crucifiers so that he was left naked, exposed to the mocking crowds (Matt. 27:35).

- *Joshua* received a splendid turban placed on his head. *Jesus* was crowned with thorns, which were pressed down into his forehead until the blood ran down his face (Matt. 27:29).

- *Joshua* was judged and declared clean on the basis of God's choice of him for salvation, found not guilty of defilement that was really his. *Jesus* was judged by sinners, found guilty on trumped up charges, and handed over to his enemies to be scourged and spat upon and put to death for defilement that was *not* his (Matt. 27:11–30). Yet this too was because of God's choice (Acts 4:28).

- *Joshua's* sin was taken away: he was declared innocent, able to stand before God as high priest for his people, bearing their name before God in the Holy of Holies. *Jesus*, who had committed no sin, was made sin by God (2 Cor. 5:21). As a result, he was separated from God the Father by that burden to the point that he cried out in agony in the darkness, "My God, my God, why have you forsaken me?" (Matt. 27:46).

There is the reality to whom Joshua pointed: it is Jesus on the cross, the one whose inscription read in truth, "This is Jesus, the king of the Jews" (Matt. 27:37). He is the one through whose death the sins of his people were truly removed in a single day. He is the one through whose death we are restored to fellowship with God, fellowship with our neighbors, and the blessings of a restored creation.

But Jesus is no longer on the cross. Now he has been raised up from the dead, clothed in glory, crowned in honor, and given the name that is above every name. Now he has ascended to the Father's right hand as our heavenly high priest, effectively interceding for us before the very throne of God. Now whenever Satan accuses you, Jesus Christ responds: "Objection! This client's sin has been paid for on my back. I was burned for him! I bled for her! God has chosen them." God the Father responds in turn: "Objection sustained! Let this one come in! There is *now no condemnation* for this brand snatched from the fire, for it has all been nailed to the cross with Christ. Nothing more can ever be laid to their account."

What is more, God is sanctifying those he has justified. The sin that mars your life now will not remain forever. The filth that so fills our hearts and disfigures our churches' beauty will not be the end of the story. The goal of Christ's work of salvation is a pure, spotless, radiant bride, able to stand in his presence forever. The church will be finally sanctified, and so will each of us individually. Sin shall *not* have dominion over us. No one and nothing can prevent it, for it is the will of God for all those who are his. The One who has begun this work in you will not rest until he has brought it to completion (Phil. 1:6).

So it is that the good news of the gospel comes to trembling sinners, to those who know their own hearts and who know how astonishing it is that a holy God should not instantly obliterate them. God welcomes you into his presence in the gospel: "There is no condemnation for you any longer! Come on in! You are welcome, beloved son, dear daughter, for the sake of Jesus Christ. Don't listen any longer to the lies of Satan when he tells you that someone like you can't approach God. Look at the cross, where my wrath was poured out and fully expended on my Son."

What is more, God also calls you to holiness in the gospel. The good news challenges you to learn to live a life that is in line with the gospel, a life that is worthy of the calling you have received. It teaches you to walk in God's ways and keep the charge that he has assigned to you in your particular situation in life. It calls you to expend every effort in pursuing holiness, not because you think you can thereby become good enough to win God's favor, but because you know that God's will is for your holiness. God has promised that one day he will produce it in you, and so you long for it and begin to strive with all your heart toward it even now.

Most of all, however, the gospel urges you to come into God's presence with joy. Feel the welcome that is yours for Christ's sake. Enjoy the freedom that comes with worshipping God with a clear conscience, which is exactly what you were made to do in the first instance! Praise God for clothing you in the beauty of his holiness, and look forward to the day when you and all of his people will sit down at his table for that great and final feast in the company of Jesus. On that day, we will be made clean once and for all, gloriously arrayed in garments of his holiness, crowned with the beauty of his splendor, and overflowing with thankfulness to him for our great salvation.

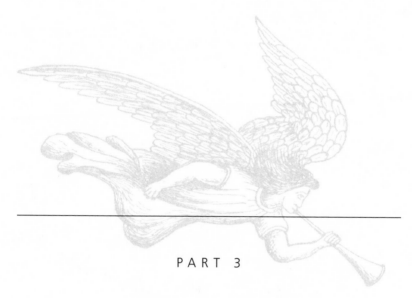

PART 3

THE PSALMS

8

BEAUTY IN THE SAND

Psalm 90

William Edgar

Introduction

While I believe I have developed my own distinctive style of preaching, Edmund Clowney left his indelible mark on me, as he did on a generation of preachers. The sermon, "Beauty in the Sand," reflects a number of those traits. Ed always began his sermons with a memorable story, or a memorable image. His marvelous message on "The Prodigal Son" (Luke 15:11–32) begins with the illustration about the town that flung out the banner to welcome home their son, a young soldier returning from the Vietnam War. His sermon, "The Singing Christ" (Psalm 22) begins with a self-deprecating story about how no one has ever asked him to sing a solo (the sermon ends where the psalm does, with Christ leading all God's people in a heavenly choir). These opening illustrations serve several purposes. Of course, they invite the attention of the congregation. But

149

more than "hooks," they are germane to the rest, and often surface throughout the message.

So my introductory story about the brave Huguenots of Le Chambon did get the attention of the congregation, especially since they were in a historic Huguenot church in New Paltz, New York. Many in the assembly had Huguenot ancestry. But the story of the *chambonnais* serves to illustrate the central point of the sermon, which is about how affliction in the desert can be turned around to become beautiful work. One needs to be careful and not let the illustration dominate the sermon in an imbalanced way. I worried that after the service people would thank me for reminding them of their ancestry or the story of the noble Huguenots of old and leave it at that. A few did remark on the Huguenots, but were able to place it in a larger setting. To be fair, the message came at the end of a field trip to New Paltz, so a strong emphasis on history was not altogether out of place.

Where Ed's influence can be most keenly felt, I trust, is in the insights gained from biblical theology into this passage. As I remember classes in Homiletics with Ed, he would require that we begin by thoroughly digging into the passage at hand, understanding it in its immediate horizon. This means knowing the literary structure, the Hebrew text, the story of Moses, the reason the people were condemned to wander in the desert, and so forth. Then we were required to look at the larger horizon. Among other things, then, I looked for themes highlighted in the passage that find their precedent and their fulfillment elsewhere in the Bible. For example, the desert is a major motif in the Scriptures. It is a real place, but also a metaphor. The desert often signifies judgment. Lack of life means the absence of the life-giver. Lack of life means lack of a living environment. The desert is unfriendly, it harkens back to the dawn of creation when nothing had form. When Jeremiah speaks of judgment, he will refer to a reversal of the order of the days of creation (Jer. 4:23). Back to the *tohu wabohu* of the world before it was habitable by mankind (Gen. 1:2).

In contrast, a theme that is highlighted as the great answer to the desert is God as a dwelling place (Ps. 90:1). Death is God's curse in the first place, which is why we return to dust (v. 3). God exposes our secret sins (v. 8). But this same God provides the answer. He it is who gives us the wisdom to number our days (v. 12). He it is we beg to return (v. 13). These themes can be found throughout the Bible. Of course, it is important not to let oneself travel endlessly into the terrain of themes and recurring subjects simply to show off one's ability to find parallels! A few key examples should suffice.

The place where Ed would have wanted his students strongly to end up is presenting Jesus Christ, the "yes and amen" of God's promises, to the congregation. What I try to do in the sermon is show how this Christ went through the desert, literally when being tempted of the devil, but also figuratively while enduring so much suffering; and because of this he can then lead us out of our deserts, whatever they might be, and into God's favor. Because the power of God's anger was turned away from us and poured out on his Son, Jesus, on the cross, we may be free from guilt, and our prayer for God's favor will be answered.

That answer comes by turning from our homelessness in the desert to our true home in God. He has been our dwelling place. His refuge is more sure than even the lush, fruitful haven of the garden. What ultimately matters is not our work, but God's work. It is his favor, his glorious power that we seek. It's a matter of seeing the world right side up.

When that is the case, then everything has meaning. The prayer is answered by making beautiful the work of our hands, even in the raw adversity of the desert. Our hands were made dirty through sin. Think of the way we literally craft idols. Or the way we shake our hands at our neighbor, or at God himself. Or, more figuratively, the hundreds of ways we engage in sleight of hand. But now, because Jesus had his own hands (and his feet) pierced, the work of our hands can be redeemed. As Paul reminds the Ephesians, no longer do thieves need to steal, but they work honestly with their hands, in order to be generous to others (Eph. 4:28). From greedy hands to helping hands!

One area I have tried to develop, which was not as strong in Ed's messages as it could have been, is personal applications. For example, the "deserts" we endure can include the agony of aging, of disease, of financial loss. Death in the desert is more than simply physical extinction. It includes all the wrenching separations in our lives, in the absence of God.

Coming back to the story of Le Chambon, I want to end where I began, and bring unity to the message. It is clear that the strength of those who resisted the Nazis came from their own desert experience, quite literally in the seventeenth century, and then in other forms thereafter. Having been forged on the anvil of suffering, their character was strong, strong enough to help others without a care for their own safety (Rom. 5:4). Behind that, of course, is Jesus, who suffered and was tempted, and therefore could help those who are tempted (Heb. 2:18). Thus, in faithfulness to all Ed taught us, I have tried to lift up Jesus Christ, clothed in the gospel, "Our God, our help in ages past, our hope for years to come."

The Scripture (Psalm 90)[1]

> Lord, you have been our dwelling place in all generations.
>> Before the mountains were brought forth,
> or ever you had formed the earth and the world,
>> from everlasting to everlasting you are God.
> You return man to dust
>> and say, "Return, O children of man!"
> For a thousand years in your sight
>> are but as yesterday when it is past,
>> or as a watch in the night.
> You sweep them away as with a flood; they are like a dream,
>> like grass that is renewed in the morning:
> in the morning it flourishes and is renewed;
>> in the evening it fades and withers.
> For we are brought to an end by your anger;
>> by your wrath we are dismayed.
> You have set our iniquities before you,
>> our secret sins in the light of your presence.
> For all our days pass away under your wrath;
>> we bring our years to an end like a sigh.
> The years of our life are seventy,
>> or even by reason of strength eighty;
> yet their span is but toil and trouble;
>> they are soon gone, and we fly away.
> Who considers the power of your anger,
>> and your wrath according to the fear of you?

1. Unless otherwise indicated, Scripture citations in this sermon are from the ESV.

So teach us to number our days
    that we may get a heart of wisdom.
Return, O LORD! How long?
    Have pity on your servants!
Satisfy us in the morning with your steadfast love,
    that we may rejoice and be glad all our days.
Make us glad for as many days as you have afflicted us,
    and for as many years as we have seen evil.
Let your work be shown to your servants,
    and your glorious power to their children.
Let the favor of the Lord our God be upon us,
    and establish the work of our hands upon us;
    yes, establish the work of our hands!

The Sermon

Le Chambon-sur-Lignon is a modest village in the middle of France
that distinguished itself during the Second World War by harbor-
ing and protecting some five thousand refugees from the Nazis.
Most of them Jews, many of them children, they were saved from
sure death in the darkest hour of European history. The wonderful
documentary done on this episode, *Weapons of the Spirit*, is directed
by Pierre Sauvage, a man born during the war in that village thanks
to the kindness of his parents' protectors. He needed to know what
gave this populace such courage. They lived in constant danger of
raids. Of modest means, these extraordinary people doubled the
size of the village in a short time. Farmers, school teachers, mer-
chants . . . one had to look for clues as to why they allowed their
town to double in size, go nearly bankrupt, live in fear of the Nazis
for five years, and do so gladly. They took in families, teenagers,
little children, placing them in their homes and welcoming them
in the local schools.

What he found out is simply astonishing. They did not consider
themselves heroes at all. They were simply obeying God, who says
we must love him and love our neighbors. As he probed deeper,
though, he found out that most of them were Huguenot Christians,
French Protestants with a remarkable history. They had character
and quiet strength, more so, sadly, than many other French people
during the war. It turns out their spirit owed a great deal to their
heritage. For their ancestors' strength was forged in the desert, quite

literally. And they well understood persecution and prejudice, for such was their own plight. That memory was passed down in song, in devotional practices, and through the preached Word.

Sixteen eighty-five was not a good year for religious liberty. After a century of a working relationship between Huguenots and the political establishment in France, things began to fall apart. Despite attempts to reunite, it simply was not going to happen. Not for lack of trying. There were remarkable cases where Roman Catholic bishops were even willing to change their own liturgy by removing prayers to the Virgin and the adoration of images, and to consider giving communion in both elements to the congregants, in order to accommodate the Protestants. But things kept going wrong. Many factors contributed to the move to eradicate Protestants from a country that claimed to be enlightened.

The king certainly played a role. Louis XIV, the "Sun King," had decided not to give any special favors to the Reformed people. Yet he could only have done this because of pressure from the grass roots. A fund was established to pay clergy if they could persuade Protestants to convert back to the Church of Rome. Prestigious jobs were promised Huguenots if they would come back to the fold. If not, various professions were denied them altogether, including the law, baking, apothecary arts, and surgery. Then it happened. After nearly a century of coexistence under the Edict of Nantes, the statute was declared void. At a meeting in Fontainebleau, in October of 1685, more than three hundred years ago, a new edict was written nullifying the rights of what they pejoratively called the RPR (*Religion Prétendue Réformée*). All their churches were to be destroyed. So were any homes where they might hold meetings. Soldiers were allowed to quarter in Protestant homes and rule the house. Any man caught preaching would be sent to the galley ships to row himself to death. Women were sent to cold and dank prisons. Their schools were abolished. Baptism in the Roman Catholic Church was required. For the more obstinate, their children were taken from them and placed in Catholic convents.

Here is how all of this relates to our text today: this was the beginning of the period known by French Protestants as "the desert." Thousands fled to foreign countries, particularly England, Ireland,

South Africa, Russia, Sweden, and, of course, Germany and America. That is why this community of New Paltz exists! The rest stayed and literally experienced the desert. Nestled in the Cévennes mountains in the South West of France, the Huguenots had to worship secretly. They carried wine barrels on donkeys' backs, which opened into pulpits to amplify the sound of the preaching. Women hid small psalters in their "chignons" (hence the fashion, until recently, favoring that hairstyle). In short, these extraordinary people had been severely tested. And they came out like gold. The gold did not fade, it shined right through the darkness of Nazi-occupied France.

⊱—⊷⊶—○—⊷⊶—⊰

The desert in the Bible is both a reality and a symbol of *judgment*. The world was made in six days, progressing from the empty, shapeless *tohu wabohu* to the lush garden. Eden was superintended by the crown of creation: human beings made as God's image. Then things went terribly wrong, and our ancestors were banished from the garden. The ground out of which man was made would reclaim him and all of his lineage. For his crime of fratricide Cain was condemned to wander on an inhospitable earth. Over and over, God's rebellious people are sent into the desert to wander. Indeed, often when the Bible speaks of judgment, it describes the reversal of the days of creation, back to the disorder, back to the desert. Consider the prophecy of Jeremiah: "I looked on the earth, and behold, it was without form and void . . . I looked, and behold, the fruitful land was a desert . . . before the LORD, before his fierce anger" (Jer. 4:23–26). The desert is thus not a natural place. For some of us there is an exotic beauty in the desert. But biblically this is a place of banishment. No, God who made the lush beauty of the earth now "turns rivers into a desert, springs of water into thirsty ground, a fruitful land into a salty waste, because of the evil of its inhabitants" (Ps. 107:33–34).

We know something of the setting for this ninetieth psalm, the only one attributed to Moses. Though gloriously delivered from bondage in Egypt, God's people had turned their hearts against him. They turned to idols, they complained about hardships, about food, and about Moses' qualifications. The sad result, as we know, was God's condemnation to wander for an entire generation in the desert (Numbers 13–17). Yes, the desert!

In a way, the human condition can be compared to living in the wilderness. Every one of us has known desert-like troubles. What kinds of deserts are you troubled by today? Is it a relative turning on you? Is it finance? Disease? Or is it numbing anxiety about the world? Is it aging? Most of the time we live without thinking much about mortality. I will never forget the first time it struck me that I was going to die. I had always known it intellectually. But one morning at a colloquium in Aix-en-Provence, where I used to teach, we had the leading French expert on genetics come and address us. I don't remember anything else he said, but he mentioned that death was written into our genetic make-up. I am not sure why, and I don't really know if he is right, but then it hit me: one day, it will happen to me.

The Bible is the most realistic book ever composed. Though ultimately full of hope, it reminds us on every page that we are but dust. There is great irony and great tragedy here. Being made from the dust of the earth is, in the Ancient Near East, a symbol of enthronement. Now in death we have lost our kingly rule. "You return man to dust," our psalm tells us, because of God's condemnation (v. 3). Think of it! We were meant to live forever, and rule over the earth, but now we are simply swept away "in the sleep of death." We are no better than the grass of the desert whose lifespan is exactly one day (v. 6).

Read these powerful words. They are a litany of suffering under God's curse. Neither Jean-Paul Sartre nor Friedrich Nietzsche could match the dark eloquence of these words. Our iniquities are exposed, and so we finish our years in moaning. There is absolutely nothing good about death. It is the great obscenity. Simply put, death is the end of our decades of misery.

⋗−⬦−◯−⬦−⋖

It is, but there is much, much more. However powerful and realistic about evil it is, the Bible also even more powerfully proclaims hope. Where can it be found? Right in this text. Remember that this psalm is a prayer. Moses addresses these sobering words not primarily to the people, but to God. The opening lines give us the resolution for the dissonances of the rest. The Lord himself is our dwelling place (v. 1). Not the desert. Nor even the land of Canaan. This same God who made everything, including the *tohu wabohu*, is our home. And he has been all along. Because "from everlasting to everlasting, [he is] God" (v. 2). Yes, he turns us back to the dust. Yes, he allows deserts in our lives, but that is to teach us to look up!

Many of our troubles come from assuming that what is only fleeting is permanent, with no escape. How often do we look at our present circumstance, with its particular troubles, and imagine that here is our real home? "I am defined by my infirmity." "I will never pull out of debt." "My colleague will never truly be my friend." "The poor you will always have with you." But this view is upside down!

The God of Moses, our God, is a special kind of God. He is one we may appeal to. We may cry out to him, and he will come through! We can ask him to relent. And he will (v. 13). Most of all, we may ask him to "satisfy us in the morning with [his] unfailing love." And he will. We may ask him to put a song in our hearts, and he will (v. 14). We may ask him to make us glad for as many days as he has afflicted us, and he will do far more. For "the free gift is not like the trespass" (Rom. 5:15). So our true dwelling place is not the desert, but the Lord himself.

How can he offer this homecoming? We know it, but we can never hear it enough. God is love. Being a loving God does not require him to save. But his decision to save introduces us to the great depths of his love. God has had compassion on his people, despite their folly. Because he loves them. Why? Because he loves them. Such matchless love, such amazing grace led him to devise a way, an unspeakably costly way, to cover our sins, to lift us from the dust and bring us into a new home, the heavenly places. He sent his only Son to suffer a horrifying death, and then to rise victorious over all of evil, including our various deserts. Indeed, inasmuch as Adam failed the test in the garden, and inasmuch as the Hebrew people failed the test in the desert, Jesus was sent to a much harsher desert, where he met Satan himself, and where weakened and sorely tempted, he emerged triumphant. More than God's people, he was hungry; but he refused to turn the stones into bread at Satan's pleasure. More than the people, he longed to exercise his power to regain the splendor of the world's cities, but not by treason. More than the people, he longed for prophecy to be fulfilled, but not on the Devil's timetable. When Jesus emerged victorious, he preached the kingdom, the realm of God's righteous presence, and invited us in.

When we turn to God for help, we find love. No other philosophy, no other religion comes remotely close. Yet we must accept this love on his own terms. His is a "severe mercy." His timing is not our timing. It is far better. The spiritual says it so well: "God don't come when you want him to, but he's always right on time." Does that mean we sit around and wait, doing nothing until the Master returns? Of course not. Moses here asks God for wisdom for today.

That wisdom, among other things, helps us number our days (v. 12). Only with age am I getting a grasp on this wonderful virtue. When I was a young man, a new believer, I came to my earthly dwelling places well armed with strategies that, so I thought, should change the world in my generation. When it did not seem to happen, I began to ask what went wrong. Simply put, I was not wise enough to number my days. Put negatively, I had not counted on how fragile things were, how short life really is. Put positively, I was not planning with proper deference to God's good providence. I am slowly acquiring the eyes to see all this. And I can say that I have seen some wonderful changes, most of which I would not have predicted forty years ago. Meanwhile, I can keep busy with a good conscience. I am slowly learning that God's favor (his beauty!) will rest upon us, and that the work of our hands may be established. This is the wise man's house built on the rock and not the sand.

><+>·O·<+><

These hands! Among the most beautiful parts of the human body, are they not? With them we bless others, we build beautiful things, including homes. We cuddle our children, we embrace friends. Conductors guide orchestras to articulate glorious symphonic sounds. And yet, how we have dirtied them. It is with our hands we forge idols. With our hands we touch what ought not to be touched (in the computer age, we "click" what ought not to be clicked). With the hand we plunge the knife into our brother's side. With our hands we curse and rail. We shake our fists against the heavens.

Consider the depths of God's love. Jesus was willing to have his most lovely hands pierced for our sakes. And his feet. And his side. Think of it. The hands by which the worlds were made; the hands that conduct angel choirs; the hand extended to the synagogue ruler's dead twelve-year-old daughter, as he tenderly said, "*talitha cumi!*" ("little girl, I say to you, arise"). Those very hands were pierced through with great cruelty at Calvary. The Son of God would be scarred forever. For our sake. He took the code written against us and nailed all its condemnations against us on the cross, through his own bloody hands canceling our debt, forgiving all our sins.

And now—praise God!—in Christ, we can be different. Here in the desert we can do lots of good. With our hands! We may lift them up in praise. Do you know the Luce Chapel in Taiwan? It was designed by I. M. Pei, and modeled after Dürer's *Praying Hands*. Not only lovely churches, but the whole earth lifts up its hands to the praise of God. The trees clap their hands in heavenly rhythm, leading God's people into the beauty of holiness.

With our hands we may embrace our fellow saints. We may reach out to those who have nothing. Let the thief steal no longer, Paul tells the Ephesians, but let him work, "doing honest work with his own hands, so that he may have something to share with those in need" (Eph. 4:28).

Of course, we may come to this place even without physical hands. I often think of Joni Eareckson Tada. When she took that fateful dive into the shallow waters of the Chesapeake Bay, she became a quadriplegic for life. Confined to the hospital for two years, she knew loneliness, darkness, grief, and despair. But lying face down, strapped onto the Stryker frame (a device allowing patients to turn in various directions without having to move their own muscles), she re-read a book that had made a mark on her in college: Victor Frankl's *Man's Search for Meaning*. She turned its pages with a mouth-stick grasped between her teeth. A Jewish psychiatrist, he had been sent to concentration camp during Word War II, and literally stripped of everything. But he found that one thing the Nazis could not take away was hope. Joni began to think about her own shattered life, and to count a few of the bright-shining threads: "I'm alive. I can at least still feel in my neck and tops of my shoulders. I can see the moon through the hospital window. I am learning that patience and endurance means more on a Stryker frame than running twenty-five laps around a hockey field. My friends are still coming to see me, and the doughnuts they bring taste good. . . . "[2]

These thoughts are the farthest thing from escapism, or Pollyanna's dreams. Indeed, Joni would go on to become one of the most powerful voices in the world for the disabled. But it all began on a Stryker frame, a sort of cross, from which she saw the world right-side up. Dear friend, come to Jesus, come to that cross, where everything was made right!

Rabbi Jonathan Sacks once remarked, "We are uniquely a meaning-seeking animal. Our most fundamental questions are Who am I? and To which narrative do I belong?"[3] He went on to say that the great hope of the liberal imagination—that economics can give us answers, that private choice is sacrosanct—this hope was bound to fail. Only in religion—we would say "*true* religion"—can there be any meaningful hope. Indeed only in this true God, a God of holy anger against evil, against our own evil, but a God of infinite mercy and goodness, can our lives have meaning and hope. Dear friend, come to this God. Give up your hopeless humanism. Find rest in Jesus' easy yoke!

When we have trained in this difficult desert, then may we even rejoice in our sufferings, knowing that suffering produces perseverance, and perseverance character, and character hope, a hope that "maketh not ashamed" (Rom. 5:3–5, KJV). Only when driven by this hope, driven, indeed, by the love of God in our hearts, poured out by the Holy Spirit, can we have the simple courage to die for other people. True for the French Huguenots of Le Chambon, it can be true of any of God's people who know they are in the desert, but who find their dwelling place not in the sand, but in the Lord who satisfies with unfailing love, who rests his beauty upon us forever.

2. Joni Eareckson Tada, *When Is It Right to Die? Suicide, Euthanasia, Suffering, Mercy* (Grand Rapids, MI: Zondervan, 1992), 84.

3. Jonathan Sacks, *The Dignity of Difference: How to Avoid the Clash of Civilizations* (New York: Continuum, 2003), 41.

For you see, marvelous as our good deeds will be when he enables them, it is God himself we desire above all else. He is indeed our dwelling place, but he is also our friend, our first love, the one who longs to have us know him and enjoy him, as he knows and enjoys us!

> Our God, our help in ages past,
> Our hope for years to come,
> Our shelter from the stormy blast,
> And our eternal home.[4]
>
> *Amen.*

---

4. Isaac Watts's paraphrase of Psalm 90:1 (1719).

PART 4

THE NEW COVENANT

9

WHEN GOD PROMISES THE IMPOSSIBLE

Luke 1:5–25

Dennis E. Johnson

Introduction

I preached this sermon to New Life Presbyterian Church, in Escondido, California, on October 29, 2000, at the beginning of a series in the Gospel of Luke, which was timed to reach the account of Jesus' birth on Sunday, December 24. I am an associate pastor in this congregation and had been serving as part-time interim pastor since the senior pastor's resignation the previous December. In consultation with our congregation's elders I had preached series of sermons addressing various congregational needs in our time of transition. By autumn 2000 we concluded that our members, friends, and visitors were ready for a return to our regular homiletic diet, a *lectio continua* series that would take us, week-by-week, through the riches of truth and grace in a particular biblical book.

165

The Gospel of Luke seemed to be an appropriate choice for a longer expository series. In a time of transition in human leadership, it is particularly crucial for God's people to have their hearts and minds drawn again and again to the ever-living, ever-present, almighty, abounding-in-mercy "Great Shepherd of the sheep," Jesus, who remains "the same yesterday, today, and forever" (Heb. 13:20, 8).[1] Since Jesus is, obviously, the "center stage" actor in the Gospel narratives, preaching through one of the four Gospels was a natural choice. Moreover, preaching Luke's Gospel would deepen our congregation's appreciation for the unity of the Bible and its witness to Christ.

New Life Presbyterian Church, located in a suburban/semi-rural community thirty miles north of San Diego, California, was established about 1980. The congregation, which numbered in the mid-two hundreds in 2000, exhibits some racial-ethnic and socio-economic diversity, although the majority is non-Hispanic Caucasian and employed in technical fields, business, education, and the professions. (The congregation also hosts in its facility a Spanish-speaking Presbyterian Church in America congregation, Misión Vida Nueva.) The "personality" of New Life Presbyterian Church is formed by the passion of its leaders and members to see our unchurched (and other non-Christian) neighbors and friends exposed to the good news of Christ in a clear and winsome way. Our worship and our preaching are therefore influenced by a desire to communicate intelligibly to a wide spectrum of listeners, avoiding the use of "in crowd" theological jargon where possible (or explaining such terms, when we use them). Another formative factor is the presence of Westminster Seminary California in Escondido, and therefore the participation of some of the seminary's faculty and students in the congregation and its ministries. So as I have looked out from the pulpit to view the folks gathered for worship at New Life on a particular Sunday, I have seen new adult Christians and mature believers (including, for nine years, Dr. and Mrs. Clowney); physicians and farmers; construction workers and computer technicians; brothers and sisters

---

1. See "An Ever Living, Never Leaving Leader," a sermon on Hebrews 13:5–14 preached to various churches soon after the departure of a pastor, printed in Appendix B of my *Him We Proclaim: Preaching Christ from All the Scriptures* (Phillipsburg, NJ: P&R, 2007), 422–32.

from the Philippines, Mexico, Uganda, Korea, Singapore, and elsewhere; children, adolescents, young families, and senior citizens.
What this miniature "assembly of the nations" needs to hear is the
message of God's redemptive plan revealed throughout Scripture
and fulfilled in Jesus the Son, articulated clearly and concretely, and
applied with gracious boldness—a challenging balance to maintain
week in and week out! New Life, for its variety of educational and
spiritual backgrounds, is a congregation accustomed to—how to say
it?—"meaty" sermons, and as a preacher I am also an "incorrigible"
teacher. This sermon is therefore somewhat longer (forty-five minutes or so) than I might preach in other settings, with more lines of
connection drawn between this passage and other Scriptures than I
might have called attention to for a different audience.

The legacy of Dr. Clowney is exhibited in this sermon in those
lines of connection between Luke's account of the annunciation of
John the Baptist's birth, on the one hand, and Old Testament history,
prophecy, and hope, on the other. The angel Gabriel's allusion to the
promise that closes Malachi's prophecy, concerning a return of Elijah to restore and prepare God's people before the day of the Lord,
is unmistakable. The parallels between the age and barrenness of
Zechariah and Elizabeth on the one hand, and Abraham and Sarah
on the other, though less overtly signaled by verbal echoes (but
compare Gabriel's promise to Mary in Luke 1:37 with God's rhetorical question to Abraham [and Sarah] in Gen. 18:14), is another
undeniable strand, I believe, binding Old Testament anticipation to
New Testament fulfillment, and specifically in the forerunner sent
ahead of the Lord to prepare Israel for his advent.

Of course faithful redemptive-historical preaching, as exemplified in the apostolic preaching found in the New Testament and
advocated and modeled by Dr. Clowney, is more than a matter
of drawing interesting intertextual links between Israel's ancient
Scriptures and the Christian church's foundational documents. Our
concern is to "preach *Christ* in all the Scriptures," for heralds of
the King are commissioned to declare the good news of salvation
through the grace of Jesus the God-man, who is both the saving
Lord and the obedient and suffering Servant of the Lord. In this
text and sermon the focus on Jesus is explicit in Gabriel's announce-

ment of John's mission to "go on *before the Lord* . . . to make ready a people prepared *for the Lord*" (Luke 1:17). It seemed appropriate and necessary, however, to put this terse "mission statement" into the context of the Gospels' elaboration of John's ministry and message. In particular, we needed to anticipate texts to be preached in coming months, in which Zechariah's son identifies Jesus as the One who would baptize with the Holy Spirit and with fire (Luke 3:16); and also to bring into view—especially in view of our passage's stress on John's priestly ancestry—the passage in another Gospel, in which John acclaims Jesus "the Lamb of God, who takes away the sin of the world" (John 1:29).

These parallels within the Gospels "tease out" the implications of the angel's description of John's calling to bring Israel back to the Lord their God, and "to turn . . . the disobedient to the obedience of the righteous." These diagnoses of human need for rescue and restoration, the redemption that Christ would come—now, has come—to achieve, should prevent our hearers from sitting aloof as third-party observers. Rather, we discover that, beneath the superficial differences of cultural and political setting, Israel's need and Zechariah's need "in the time of Herod king of Judea," are reflective of our deepest spiritual need: to be turned back toward the Lord who made us, our sin atoned for by the blood of the Lamb and our hearts transformed by the washing of the Spirit. A sober exposé of our own unbelief, as visible in the doubt of "upright" Zechariah, prepares our hearts to savor the sweetness of God's grace in the gospel of his Son, the Lord who is the Lamb.

The Scripture (Luke 1:5–25)[2]

In the time of Herod king of Judea there was a priest named Zechariah, who belonged to the priestly divison of Abijah; his wife Elizabeth was also a descendant of Aaron. Both of them were upright in the sight of God, observing all the Lord's commandments and regulations blamelessly. But they had no children, because Elizabeth was barren; and they were both well along in years.

2. Unless otherwise identified, Scripture citations in this sermon are from the NIV.

Once when Zechariah's division was on duty and he was serving as priest before God, he was chosen by lot, according to the custom of the priesthood, to go into the temple of the Lord and burn incense. And when the time for the burning of incense came, all the assembled worshipers were praying outside.

Then an angel of the Lord appeared to him, standing at the right side of the altar of incense. When Zechariah saw him, he was startled and was gripped with fear. But the angel said to him: "Do not be afraid, Zechariah; your prayer has been heard. Your wife Elizabeth will bear you a son, and you are to give him the name John. He will be a joy and delight to you, and many will rejoice because of his birth, for he will be great in the sight of the Lord. He is never to take wine or other fermented drink, and he will be filled with the Holy Spirit even from birth. Many of the people of Israel will he bring back to the Lord their God. And he will go on before the Lord, in the spirit and power of Elijah, to turn the hearts of the fathers to the children, and the disobedient to the wisdom of the righteous—to make ready a people prepared for the Lord."

Zechariah asked the angel, "How can I be sure of this? I am an old man and my wife is well along in years."

The angel answered, "I am Gabriel. I stand in the presence of God, and I have been sent to speak to you and to tell you this good news. And now you will be silent and not able to speak until the day this happens, because you did not believe my words, which will come true at their proper time."

Meanwhile, the people were waiting for Zechariah, and wondering why he stayed so long in the temple. When he came out, he could not speak to them. They realized he had seen a vision in the temple, for he kept making signs to them but remained unable to speak.

When his time of service was completed, he returned home. After this his wife Elizabeth became pregnant and for five months remained in seclusion. "The Lord has done this for me," she said. "In these days he has shown his favor and taken away my disgrace among the people."

The Sermon

When I was a kid, one line in the carol, "Hark! The Herald Angels Sing," always bothered me: "*Late* in time behold Him come, offspring of the Virgin's womb."[3] It always seemed disrespectful to sing that Jesus had arrived "late," that he had somehow forgotten to set his alarm or check his calendar, that the "Lord of years" had missed his scheduled appointment or the opening bell for school, that the Sovereign of seasons and seconds deserves a tardy. Well, I admit it: I do remember that as a child I felt—as all American children do, I think—that Christmas would take *forever* to arrive every year. But still I wondered, should we be singing that Jesus came "late" to bring the salvation we need?

I eventually made peace with "Hark the Herald Angels Sing" by thinking of that line as meaning that Jesus arrived "late*ly*"—*recently*, not so long ago. That was still a stretch for us to sing 2000 years after his birth, or even for Charles Wesley to write in the eighteenth century. The birth in Bethlehem during the reign of Caesar Augustus seems to belong to a distant past, not "late breaking news." But at least if we understand "late" as "lately," we are not criticizing God's timetable for sending the Savior into the world.

And yet, whatever Wesley may have meant by that uncomfortable adverb "late," the more I think about it, the more I believe that to a lot of people when Jesus was born and in the centuries before, the arrival of the Messiah must have seemed awfully long in coming. Surely they must have wondered, *has God missed his appointment? Has he forgotten his promise?* Often in the Psalms we hear Israel's singers lament, "How long, O Lord, until you come to our rescue, until you set us free from oppression and injustice, from suffering and death?" The singer of Psalm 89 laments, "How long, O LORD? Will you hide yourself forever? How long will your wrath burn like fire? Remember how fleeting is my life . . . " (vv. 46–47). Another almost shouts, "Awake, O Lord! Why do you sleep? Rouse yourself! Do not reject us forever!" (Ps. 44:23).

And this confusion or frustration over God's delay is not just a dilemma that troubled ancient Israelites. Even after Jesus came to earth, died, rose from the dead, and ascended to heaven with a promise to return some day, even while the apostles were alive,

3. Charles Wesley, "Hark! the Herald Angels Sing" (1739). I could also have mentioned the line in "O Come, All Ye Faithful," which speaks of Jesus as "Word of the Father, *late* in flesh appearing" (from the Latin hymn *Adeste Fideles*; English words attributed to John Francis Wade, 1751).

people were grumbling, "Where is this coming he promised?" (2 Pet. 3:4). In fact, it was not only impatient doubters who wondered, *when?* In a vision in the book of Revelation we hear the lament of martyrs who were killed for trusting in Jesus, still asking, "How long, Sovereign Lord, holy and true, until you judge the inhabitants of the earth and avenge our blood?" (Rev. 6:10). In other words, when will you *finally* show the world that we were right to put our lives on the line for the hope you have promised?

It's a question that Christmas raises for a lot of people as it comes around every year: If that holiday (now just a couple months away) really commemorates the birth of God the Son, who came into the world to fix what's wrong with it and with us, why is there still so much wrong with the world and with us? What's taking him so long? American troops and Iraqi civilians, Israelis and Palestinians are killed almost daily. Wildfires sweep through southern California, flu sweeps across America, AIDS sweeps through Africa and Asia and elsewhere. Heartbreak sweeps into our lives close to home, too: loved ones die, jobs and savings disappear, people let us down and even break our hearts. Where is the "peace on earth" that the angel promised? How long do we have to wait? It's almost enough to make us give up hope, to shield our hearts from the pain of disappointment by encasing them in a callus of cynicism.

The account of Zechariah and Elizabeth that introduces Luke's story of the first Christmas is for people so tired of waiting, so hopeless and hurting, that all the superficial, sentimental holiday cheer that advertisers are already pushing at us only makes them feel worse. As Luke begins to tell the greatest story ever told, his narrative begins with a hopeless situation—actually *two* hopeless situations, one inside the other. The sorrow and regret of an elderly and childless couple mirrors in miniature the bleak situation of the whole people of God "in the time of Herod king of Judea" (Luke 1:5). If it seems to you that God is too "late," that he has missed his moment for keeping his word and bringing relief to this hurting world and your own wounded heart, then Zechariah and Elizabeth could certainly identify with your frustration and disappointment. But after their decades of waiting and praying and hoping, when their hopes had faded away, God had a surprise in store for them, an impossible promise that he would keep within months of its announcement. More than that, God's astonishing answer to prayers for which they no longer expected an answer is an integral part of his "big picture" plan to reverse misery and hopelessness at a global, even cosmic level.

But the story starts not with the joys of hope fulfilled, but rather in the anguish of hope deferred, and all but forgotten.

Heart-Wrenching Sorrow Does Not Play Favorites (vv. 5–7)

Luke opens his narrative of "the things that have been *fulfilled* among us" (1:1)—a hint of ancient prophetic promises coming into their own—by introducing an old, honorable, and pious couple who shared a deep sorrow: Zechariah, a priest serving God's sanctuary, and his wife Elizabeth.

Zechariah was in the priestly division of Abijah, one of twenty-four groups that ministered in the temple on a rotation that brought them to Jerusalem for a week at a time, twice a year—plus extra service during Israel's three great annual feasts. These divisions were set up by David in anticipation of the temple that his son Solomon would build. They had been functioning, off and on, for almost one thousand years (1 Chron. 24:1–19). Elizabeth also was descended from Aaron, Israel's high priest (Luke 1:5), so here we have a couple whose whole lives and the lives of their families for generations and generations have been bound up with Israel's worship of the living God. Today it would be like one "preacher's kid," one "PK," marrying another "PK."

Now, you may be thinking, "I have known PKs, and I have seen them react in wild rebellion against the pressures of living in the fishbowl of the parsonage, the double standard and harsher criticism that can be leveled at the pastor's family." But PK rebellion is not inevitable, and for Zechariah and Elizabeth the whole "priest's kids" experience had turned out well. We read that they were both "*upright* in the sight of God, observing all the Lord's commandments and regulations *blamelessly*" (1:6).

This is an extraordinary compliment! God's Word doesn't lightly throw around the terms "upright" and "blameless"! In fact, the Bible bluntly says that every human being except One (Jesus) is born

bent, twisted away from delighting to follow the Lord's commandments. In this very Gospel Jesus will tell a parable about a Pharisee
and a tax collector, to puncture the self-inflated balloon of "some
who were confident of their own righteousness and looked down
on everybody else . . ." (18:9).

So the very fact that Luke, writing words given to him by the
Spirit of truth, can describe both Zechariah and his wife Elizabeth
in this way sends us a signal that God's kindness to them didn't
stop when he gave them good parents. God had also softened their
hearts so that they trusted him and wanted to live by his instructions.
Notice that their blameless integrity was not just an act, a facade, a
hypocritical pretense to attract the admiration of other people. No,
they were upright *in the sight of God himself*, who looks right through
our masks to examine the secrets of our hearts.

Of course, when Luke says they followed the Lord's commands
blamelessly, he is not claiming they batted 1.000, or scored 100
percent on every test, every moment of every day. After all, in a
few sentences we will hear this "upright" Zechariah challenge a
majestic angel carrying God's own promise, demanding evidence
to bolster God's credibility. So Zechariah's "blameless" uprightness
is not absolutely unsullied purity. Still, the basic allegiance of his
and Elizabeth's hearts was oriented toward trusting, loving, and
serving their Maker.

So the description of Zechariah and Elizabeth gets better and
better: a great family pedigree, the priestly privilege of serving in
the temple, a long-lasting marriage, and oneness of heart in living
in the light of the Lord's commands. What more could they want?
Children!

Suddenly at verse 7 a cloud covers the sun: "But they had no
children, because Elizabeth was barren; and they were both well
along in years." During her child-bearing years Elizabeth had not
been able to conceive, and now both Zechariah and Elizabeth were
so old that the prospect of welcoming little ones into the world was
long gone. *Doubly impossible, doubly hopeless!*

Perhaps when you hear a sentence like this, it is like a dagger slic-
ing into your own heart. You may not be "well along in years," but
you have tried and prayed to conceive—sometimes for years—and

the Lord has not given you children. When a new pregnancy or birth is announced around here, you rejoice with others; but behind your rejoicing is always the question, Lord, why not us too?

Elizabeth would have felt the pain even more deeply in an ancient culture, where a wife's worth was measured by her ability to give her husband sons to carry his name into the future and inherit his estate. She speaks at the end of our text of "my disgrace among the people" (1:25), and who can imagine what that shame must have been like, for all those years?

Heart-wrenching sorrow does not play favorites. It does not afflict only those people who deserve pain, who defy God, who trample other people in their climb to the top, who cut corners in business, who abuse their bodies with addictions, who betray their friends, who trade in a spouse for a newer, sleeker model, or who exploit the weak. Heart-wrenching sorrow and hope-destroying disappointment touch people who love God and love other people, too.

Scripture is full of this pain. Elizabeth is just the latest in a long line of childless wives: Sarah, Rachel, Manoah's wife (from whom Samson would be born), and Hannah. The closest parallel to Elizabeth's experience was Sarah's, since neither could conceive during her childbearing years and both were well beyond those years by the time God intervened to turn their disgrace into astonished joy (Gen. 18:11–12).

As personally painful as the childlessness of Zechariah and Elizabeth was, God's Word also shows us that their family's heart-wrenching sorrow reflected an even bigger trauma that afflicted all of God's people at that time. That is why Luke sets the context with the words, "in the time of Herod king of Judea" (v. 5). Although Herod bore the title, "king of Judea," he was *not a Jew at all*, much less a descendant of David, whose dynasty was supposed to rule God's people forever. In fact, Herod was an Idumean, a descendant of the Edomites, of Israel's brother Esau.

Nor had Herod come to power or kept his grip on power through kindness to his subjects. A savvy political opportunist, Herod had recognized Julius Caesar's rising star and aided Caesar and Marc Antony in their power struggle against the Roman Senate. When Caesar finally gained the upper hand, he authorized Antony to appoint Herod as "king of the Jews." So Herod gladly showed appreciation for the pagan patrons who placed him in power over God's subjugated people. In Caesar's honor Herod built a cosmopolitan city on the coast, Caesarea Maritima, "Caesar's City-by-the-Sea." In honor of Marc Antony, Herod constructed a military fortress right in Jerusalem, overlooking the temple courtyard, perfectly placed so that Rome's occupying forces could keep a close eye on the Jews' assemblies.

Oh, it is true that Herod tried to buy his way into Jewish hearts by a costly, lengthy renovation and expansion of the temple. But amid the splendor of the Idumean's remodeled temple, his Jewish subjects still had to worship under the watchful eyes of foreign forces who occupied the Lord's land. So Luke's brief introduction, "in the time of Herod king of Judea," would speak volumes to one like "most excellent" Theophilus (1:3), who no doubt was aware of the political realities in the Roman province of Judea. "The time of Herod" was a time of Judea's shame and subjugation, a time of longing and waiting for the Lord to comfort his people and relieve their oppression.

As the people gathered outside the sanctuary, in the temple court, to pray (1:10), we can easily picture them glancing toward Herod's Fortress Antonia and praying for the Lord to lift the heavy yoke of this Edomite, this Roman puppet, from their necks. It had been a long time since God's people had been free to worship the Lord and follow his word without interference from powerful foreign idolaters! And so the people pray, even as Zechariah enters the sanctuary to burn the incense that symbolizes their prayers (Rev. 5:8). They pray for themselves, and for the people to whom they belong; for forgiveness of their sins, and for relief from their sins' bitter consequences.

We too struggle to understand why God doesn't answer prayers, at least on our timetable. Four members of our New Life family have died of cancer this year, and over the last two years cancer has snatched away two beloved elders who shepherded us so faithfully. Some of us are praying that the Lord will turn around a child who is now defiantly bent on a course of self-destruction. Some pray daily that Christ's Spirit will draw a spouse, our parents, a close sibling, friends or coworkers or neighbors out of their suicidal self-sufficiency and into the real life that only Jesus can give. Like Zechariah and Elizabeth, like Judeans under Herod, so we pray; and we wait for the Lord to hear, to wake up, to act.

God's Promise Is Too Good to Be Believed (vv. 8–17)

While the people were praying outside in the open temple court-yard, Zechariah was offering incense inside, on the altar in the Holy Place, before the heavy veil leading to the Holy of Holies (vv. 8–10). This was Zechariah's once-in-a-lifetime opportunity. For two weeks each year, the priests belonging to his division would travel to Jerusalem to serve at the temple. Historians estimate that there may have been eighteen thousand priests serving among the twenty-four divisions who rotated in attendance to the temple and its ceremonies. Of these, one priest would be chosen by lot each morning and another each evening to offer incense in the Holy Place. That's 730 priests per year, out of eighteen thousand. If casting lots operated on averages (of course they do not), each priest could have this privilege once every twenty-five years or so. This could well have been Zechariah's first and only opportunity to perform this extraordinary priestly privilege.[4]

Suddenly Zechariah is aware of a terrifying intruder: a glorious messenger from God's heavenly court, an angel standing on the right side of the incense altar. Now, in Scripture the right side signifies *blessing and favor* rather than judgment (Gen. 35:18; Ps. 110:1). Yet the appearance of the angel is apparently so overwhelming that Zechariah was "startled" and gripped with fear. Hallmark greeting card art shows angels as cute, pudgy toddlers with wings or as fragile and feathery wisps, painted in pale pastels. American entertainment media portray angels as calm, comforting nurturers, who put our petty problems into perspective with gentle advice delivered in a lilting Irish brogue. But real angels, biblical angels, send people into shock!

---

4. Descendants of Aaron did not begin their priestly service until they turned thirty years old (Num. 4:2–3, 23, 30; 1 Chron. 23:3).

But the angel says, "Do not be afraid!" And then he delivers an utterly unbelievable message (vv. 13–17): "Your prayer has gotten through. Elizabeth will bear a son" (Luke 1:13, DEJ[5]).

Now, put yourself in Zechariah's place, if you can. Think about the bizarre combination of the two statements in the angel's message. *Which* prayer of Zechariah's could the angel be referring to?

It's hard to believe that he had *just then* been praying for a son. After all, Zechariah's skeptical reaction to the angel's promise (v. 18) gives us every reason to doubt that Zechariah had been praying any time recently that God would miraculously replay the Abraham-Sarah-Isaac story, reversing Elizabeth's barrenness. Plainly, from Zechariah's perspective, God had long ago missed his chance to answer *that* prayer! God was much, much too late!

Besides, his responsibility *at that moment*, as a priest offering incense, was to pray for others, to pray for God's wounded people, not to exploit his access by bringing his personal "wish list" before the throne, seeking a privileged remedy for his and Elizabeth's private pain. Was Zechariah, then, praying for God to bring the Messiah to rescue Israel, as the people may also have been praying for freedom and relief outside (v. 10)? Is this the prayer that God has heard and is about to answer?

Or could it be that *both* prayers are in view, that *both* Zechariah's personal plea and his priestly petition for others are about to be answered? Could Zechariah's long abandoned, almost forgotten prayer for a son and his present prayer for the people's rescue be intertwined in the plan of God? Is that why the lot fell to him to offer the incense on this particular day?

As the angel elaborates, it becomes clear that God's answer to Zechariah's prayer actually will interweave divine mercy to this old man and his old wife with God's bigger plan to show mercy to many more hurting people: Your son "will be a joy and delight to you, and *many* will rejoice because of his birth" (v. 14). When God answers Zechariah's prayer for a son, he is setting in motion the promise by which he will answer *many* people's prayers for salvation. The "miracle baby" John, who will start his prophetic career *in*

---

5. Scripture citations marked DEJ are Dennis Johnson's translations or paraphrases.

utero, jumping for joy in his mother's womb even before he's born, will be the Lord's "advance team" to get things ready for the royal visit to this earth.

Zechariah's son will be filled with the Spirit, but not with alcoholic spirits (Luke 1:15). There will be no wine for John, not because God disapproves of these good gifts and the celebrations they accompany, but because John is to be an ascetic Nazirite (Num. 6:3), an austere and driven prophet, with no time for everyday life's common pleasures, pursuing an all-consuming mission from God (Luke 7:33; Mark 1:6). The deafening silence of heaven over the last four centuries, since Malachi had proclaimed God's Word to exiles resettling in Judah, was about to be broken. The Spirit of God was about to fill a man of God to declare the Word of God again.

And, just as God had promised through Malachi before he cut off communication, this new prophet, Zechariah's son, would come as a new Elijah, to return wayward rebels to their God (Mal. 4:5–6). John will bring back many Israelites to the Lord their God, and "he will turn the hearts of the fathers to the children and the disobedient to the wisdom of the righteous." Reconciliation will heal relationships between Israel and the Lord, and between fathers and children (Luke 1:16–17).

Now, we need to face head-on the implication of the mission that the angel predicts for Zechariah's son. It is this: people are *facing and moving in the wrong direction*. This is true not just about people living long ago and far away. It is what comes naturally to *every one of us*. It is our "default setting" to be turned away from God, to resent his authority and to resist his direction, and to repress the reality that we are utterly dependent on him for life itself, and for rescue from the twisted cravings of our hearts.

John's message will be that the Lord is about to come, and that coming will *not* produce joy in anyone, *unless something changes* in us. In each of us there is a deep defect that needs radical fixing. Rebels running for all their strength to escape our Creator and achieve our independence need to be brought to our senses—to "the wisdom of the righteous"—before we plunge off the cliff into eternal destruction. Our hearts need to be turned around 180 degrees, to face the

God we have been fleeing. And the bitter backwash of our past rebellion has to be neutralized somehow.

John is going to use water to say, "You need to be washed—more deeply than this water can reach, and by somebody much stronger and purer than I am. He will wash you inside—the stains on your memory and conscience—with the Holy Spirit of God" (Luke 3:16, DEJ). John will say, "This coming One who washes hearts by his Spirit is also the Lamb of God who takes away the world's sins" (John 1:29, DEJ). And when Jewish people heard John, the priest's son, talk about a Lamb taking away sins, they knew exactly *how* lambs took away sins in the temple rituals—by dying in the place of sinners (Ex. 12:6–13; 13:11–16; Isa. 53:6–7).

That Lamb—Jesus—would sacrifice himself to take away sins, to turn us around, to bring us to God the Father . . . and to turn our hearts toward each other, too—in confession and forgiveness: fathers reconciled to children, disobedient people brought around to share the wisdom of the righteous.

And the amazing thing about John's mission and message is that the *Lamb* whose sacrifice atones for sins is the *Lord* himself. John will run ahead like an imperial herald, preparing subjects in every town and city for the arrival of "the Lord their God" (Luke 1:16–17). The following record in Luke's Gospel makes clear that this coming Lord is Jesus.

But the Lord's coming brings joy *only* to a people *prepared* for what he comes to bring. John's message will announce the arrival of a Mighty Master who not only bestows God's purifying Spirit but also ignites God's consuming fire of justice (3:16). This is why John's mission was so crucial. He will run on ahead, yelling at the top of his lungs, "The King is coming! Get ready!" And this is why God's "lateness," as frustrating as it feels, is actually mercy: he will not come a moment too soon, to catch us unwarned, unaware of our danger.

Even today God is being patient, and sending preachers to get the Word out: "The King is coming back—and you don't want him to catch you unaware and unprepared when he arrives!" So that raises the question for every one of us: What direction are you facing? Toward what are you running with all your strength—the prize that you "have to have" to make your life meaningful, to make it count? Has God's Word grabbed your attention, turned you around, and brought you face to face with Jesus, the Lord who became the Lamb? When you stand some day—as we all will—before the God who reads our hidden fantasies (chilling thought!), will you meet him with joy or with dread? Even pious Zechariah needed radical heart surgery, as his next exchange with the angel shows. Neither you nor I need anything less!

God Treats Our Feeble Faith with Severe Mercy (vv. 18–22)

Here I mean "treat" in the medical sense: God administers the needed medication to heal our feeble faith, but sometimes the cure will hurt us—at least in the short term—more than the symptoms of the disease. Life-threatening cancer can sometimes be stopped by ruthless, aggressive chemotherapy; but the side effects of the treatment can be devastating on the patient. Likewise hidden spiritual malignancy—even the weary doubt of an otherwise upright saint like Zechariah—may require cure by strong and painful medicine.

Now, Zechariah's reaction to the angel's outlandish announcement seems so reasonable under the circumstances, doesn't it? After decades of God's aloof silence or forgetfulness, now to be told that you will soon father a baby at all, much less one who will change history, is, well, *just incredible*. Who wouldn't ask, "How can I be *sure* of this?" (v. 18).

Perhaps Zechariah was thinking, "After all, year after year we submitted our request in triplicate. We sent it by fax, phone, email, and certified letter, with return receipt requested. *And we heard nothing*—not 'temporarily out of stock,' not 'back ordered, to be shipped in sixty days,' not 'your credit card expired—please send a check'—but absolutely *nothing*. And *now* you expect me to leap into hope, just because an angel (admittedly, a terrifying angel) says that God ran across our order after all these years and shipped the package yesterday? Excuse me, but *is there a number I can call* to verify this offer?"

I expect that many of us understand and empathize with Zechariah's weariness over waiting and his wariness now when a terrifying emissary from heaven suddenly appears talking nonsense. Haven't you given up on some things you begged God for in the past? How long had *you* been asking? As long as Zechariah and Elizabeth? As long as Israel had been begging God to send David's royal son to set them free?

But Gabriel—now at last we learn the angel's name—does *not* consider this a reasonable question at all! So much depends on your perspective! From Zechariah's viewpoint this new hope, when all hope had died, was too astonishing to process on short notice. He needs proof. From Gabriel's viewpoint—having just come from God's radiant throne room to its earthly replica, the temple, to deliver *good news*—the reluctance of this old man, pious though he may be, to embrace God's promise is simply *inexcusable*! "Do you think I'm a *lowly messenger boy* who might have gotten the message wrong? I am Gabriel. I stand in the presence of God! I have been sent to tell you this good news. And you dare to question my integrity by demanding a sign that what I say is so and what God promises will happen?" (v. 19, DEJ).

Zechariah's demand for evidence has revealed his blindness to the distinguished rank of God's messenger. This is *Gabriel*, whose appearance in a vision to Daniel struck that ancient prophet with such terror that he dropped to the floor flat on his face (Dan. 8:16–17). This is *Gabriel*, who "stands in the presence of God" himself—an intimate member of the heavenly court among whom the Lord reigns over all. Zechariah has no excuse for doubting, no excuse for demanding any more proof than the Word of God brought by the messenger of God.

Yet Zechariah gets the evidence he feels he needs: the bittersweet sign of silence (vv. 20–22). It really is *both bitter and sweet.*

Zechariah's muteness through the next nine months of his son's gestation is *sweet* grace for two reasons. *First*, it could have been worse. Calling God a liar, or insisting on checking his references, is not smart, and could be lethal! And, *second*, Zechariah's inability to speak until John is born and named is the sign he is asking for. He seeks an immediate, miraculous confirmation of Gabriel's words, so he and Elizabeth will not go through weeks and months of waiting, only to have hopes dashed again. Well, he's got it—his tongue is tied until Gabriel's words find fulfillment, right on time (v. 20).

But this sign is also *bitter*. It is painful discipline, radical treatment to burn away a hidden malignancy of doubt and despair at the core of Zechariah's being. After John's birth, the communication frustrations over naming the baby (vv. 59–63) give a hint of what the intervening nine months may have been like between Zechariah and Elizabeth. And his inability to speak would also hinder Zechariah's ministry. When not offering sacrifice and service in the temple, a priest's other important task was to teach God's Law. Before God himself "went mute" four hundred years before, he had said through Malachi, "For the lips of a priest ought to preserve knowledge, and from his mouth men should seek instruction—because he is the messenger of the LORD Almighty" (Mal. 2:7). This Torah teaching would have been Zechariah's main occupation in his village in the Judean hills. But how could he do that without speaking? Struck mute, he now knows that God really has made a mighty promise . . . but his lips cannot find words to tell anyone about it! No wonder, when his tongue is loosened again at John's birth, Zechariah bursts forth in praise to God (Luke 1:67–79)!

Now, it is rare in the New Testament for God miraculously to inflict a *disability* on someone. Paul was struck blind, as was Elymas the magician on Cyprus (Acts 9:8–9; 13:11), but ordinarily the power of Jesus and his name is exerted to heal, not to hurt. Nevertheless, in God's wise and kind providence he does bring into each of his children's lives things that hinder, frustrate, and inhibit us. It may be health problems, or time demands, or financial need, or family turmoil, or hitting the limit of our skill or discipline or resources to pursue the vocation we have always dreamed about. It's easy for us to taste the bitter side of these things, but can we see their sweetness? Like Zechariah's inability to speak, they are tokens of God's love, pulling our hearts away from ourselves and grounding them firmly in himself. Sometimes the Lord stills and silences us through suffering, not because he is pushing us away but because he is drawing us even closer to his own heart.

God's Amazing Grace Removes Our Disgrace (vv. 23–25)

Luke closes this account not with the sounds of silence, but with an old woman's song of astonished praise, offered up to the God who replaces the ashes of despair and disgrace with the festal robes of hope and glory.

Luke is discrete about John's conception, sparing us the intimate details. He writes simply: "When his time of service was completed, [Zechariah] returned home. After this his wife Elizabeth became pregnant . . ." (vv. 23–24). In other words, Zechariah now believed God's promise, his hopes revived, and he took appropriate action on the basis of Gabriel's assurance that their marital union could and would produce a son.

Elizabeth, in privacy, worships the Lord who makes impossible promises, and then makes his impossible promises come true! She is echoing the joyful words of Rachel, Jacob's beloved but barren wife, at the birth of her son Joseph, "God has taken away my disgrace" (Gen. 30:23). And the divine grace that turned Elizabeth's disgrace into celebration made her, in microcosm, a sign that the era of barrenness for God's people was ending as well. Isaiah promised a population explosion in the tent of God's barren wife Israel:

> "Sing, O barren woman,
>   you who never bore a child;
>   burst into song, shout for joy,
>   you who were never in labor;
>   because more are the children of the desolate woman
>   than of her who has a husband," says the LORD.
> "Enlarge the place of your tent,
>   stretch your tent curtains wide,
>   do not hold back;
>   lengthen your cords,
>   strengthen your stakes.
> For you will spread out to the right and to the left;
>   your descendants will dispossess the nations
>   and settle in their desolate cities." (Isa. 54:1–3)

Now that population explosion was about to begin!

Elizabeth's aged womb, like that of Sarah centuries before, has been touched by the God who brings hope out of despair because he can bring life out of death. Both Sarah and her husband Abraham had laughed at the Lord's impossible, ridiculous promise (Gen. 17:17; 18:11–12); but the Lord got the last laugh, commanding them to name their impossible, inconceivable son . . . Isaac, "he laughs" (17:19). The apostle Paul comments on that ancient laugh-fest, in which God gave life to the dead and hope to the hopeless:

> Against all hope, Abraham in hope believed and so became the fa-ther of many nations, just as it had been said to him, "So shall your offspring be." Without weakening in his faith, he faced the fact that his body was as good as dead—since he was about a hundred years old—and that Sarah's womb was also dead. Yet he did not waver through unbelief regarding the promise of God, but was strength-ened in his faith and gave glory to God, being fully persuaded [we might be tempted to add, "at the end of the day, at least"] that God had power to do what he had promised. (Rom. 4:18–21)

The conception of Isaac in Sarah's dead womb, and then the con-ception of Joseph in Rachel's barren womb, and then the conception of John from aged Zechariah and Elizabeth are all previews of God's ultimate triumph—bringing life out of death in the resurrection of the Lord Jesus Christ.

Abraham and Sarah laughed at God's impossible promise when he made it, and then they laughed at their own feeble faith when God kept it. Luke doesn't tell us whether Zechariah had enough voice to chuckle at his own doubt as he watched his wife get bigger over the months—his prophet-son leaping and kicking, eager to get out and get on with the job of pointing people to the Messiah. But we have stronger reason to keep hoping in God's promises than Zechariah and Elizabeth did. Better than Elizabeth's expanding womb is Jesus' empty tomb, showing that he has defeated both our guilt and the death that threatens us.

Zechariah's months of silence and his subsequent song show us that when God promises the impossible, he will prove true to his Word. To us it may feel now as if Christ's second coming is "late in time," but his patience knows the perfect moment. He will not come too soon, for he is still sending messengers to prepare people to welcome his glorious appearing, to turn their hearts around through the good news of the death and resurrection of Jesus the Lamb. Has he turned you around today, to face his heart-searching purity and surrender to his grace and royal rule in humble faith?

And, in the end, we will finally realize that Jesus' return is not too late either—that no sorrow or suffering we endure, no deferred hope will prove to have been unnecessary or meaningless. Every pain and every moment of watching and waiting for the return of the King is a stylus by which God's Spirit inscribes Jesus' beauty and joy more deeply into us, his brothers and his sisters.

10

SOUL-RAVISHING
SIGHTINGS

Luke 9:28–36

Joseph F. Ryan

Introduction

My sermon file for this message is thick, far thicker than almost any other. The file has been filled over the years with quotations, clippings, and relevant notes, all on the subject of worship or on the text itself. (No, I haven't moved my sermons over to electronic filing.) The file also contains several successive versions of the sermon, each one attempting to cram in more of the supporting materials discovered since it was last preached. All this is to say that I have preached this sermon a few times over the course of ministry at the two churches I served for thirty years. It has also been one of the messages to which I have intuitively defaulted when speaking at other churches and occasions. I remember hearing Dick Lucas from St. Helen's Bishopgate in London say, "Blessed is the man who gets to preach the same sermon twice or three times." I don't think Dick said this because subsequent uses of the message might entail less preparation. Rather, repeated opportunities with the same text drive it to the heart of the preacher, so that it doesn't come from the study without going through the prayer room. Speaking for myself, since the distance from my head to my heart is the longest journey I have ever taken, I have been glad to deepen my own love for this text by returning to it more often than most others.

The Mountain of Transfiguration is all about worship. The most valuable thing in this sermon file is a collection of handouts and notes from Ed Clowney's course for first-year Westminster students on the biblical theology of worship. It was Ed who originally helped me make sense of this passage by helping me make sense of three churches where I worshiped just before or during my first year in seminary. Each was quite different from the others; each helped me experience a different emphasis in worship. The first was the high Reformed worship of Tenth Presbyterian Church in Philadelphia. The second was the warm community gathered for worship at the L'Abri Church in Huemoz, Switzerland, where I lived and studied for six months before coming to Westminster. And the third was St. Paul's, a slightly charismatic Episcopal church in my hometown of Darien, Connecticut, where I worshiped for several summers during college and seminary.

Ed helped me define what I most liked about each of these churches. Respectively, it was preaching (Tenth), community (L'Abri), and a palpable sense of God's presence and glory (St. Paul's). I spent a lot of seminary trying to think about how to get these three character- istics together in one church. Listening to Ed teach at Westminster, talking with him in many private conversations, and traveling with him as he preached in a variety of churches and settings, all shaped my own convictions about biblical worship. Several years later when Ed and Jean came to Charlottesville to join in the ministry at Trin- ity Presbyterian, I would sometimes watch Ed sitting in the con- gregation during worship, noticing his body language with some amusement when he did not particularly like something that was happening. I'm not the only one who, over the years, noticed the way he would squirm when things got a little too Anglican, too dull, too folksy, or too charismatic for him. Even Ed's squirming taught me much about worship.

Convictions about preaching, community, and glory . . . all of this background I brought to the first time I preached this text at Trinity when Ed was present. I wanted to show how worship is motivated ("compelled" may be better) by a vision of the Lord Jesus Christ on the mountain. It was important that the sermon not only be an exposition of truth (preaching), but also that it demonstrate the very truth being taught, in this case the eternal identity and beauty of the Son (glory). The Word of the Lord is most heard when the Lord of the Word is most worshiped. (You see, I can't get away from the way Ed would put things.) Only by the exposition of the Word can the beauty and glory of the Lord be seen, and only by seeing the beauty and glory of the Lord in worship can we come to the Word's deepest meaning. I wanted God's people to "taste and see" as they listened. I also wanted the people to see the corporate nature of this kind of worship, that glory is perhaps best seen in the company of other worshipers, just as Peter, James, and John were together in worship on the mountain (community). I sought for the preaching to be the "event" where the Word, the Lord, and all of us present met by the Spirit's power.

I also sought to do what Ed would always do in preaching: in this case, to show how worship is not something that started with Acts 2, but rather was rooted in Israel's earliest experiences as a people for God's own possession. In the case of this text, the obvious connection between the mountain of Horeb and that of the Trans-figuration becomes much more than interesting. The connection "makes the case" that the Transfiguration reveals "the glory of God in the face of Jesus Christ," glory shown much earlier in the burning bush, itself an event intended to prepare Israel for the greater glory to come in Christ. Ed taught us that worship, or any other New Testament occurrence, cannot be separated from the redemptive-historical events through which God led Israel. In Luke 9, the events in the background are not only the worship at Horeb but also the departure, the exodus, of the people of Israel from the tyranny of Egypt and Elijah's dramatic "departure" in the heavenly chariot. It is by bringing these Old Testament departures together with the departure that Jesus is preparing to make from Jerusalem, that the meaning of each and the significance of the latter is brought to bear on those of us who await our own departures to the freedom and glory previewed by Moses and promised by Jesus.

What Ed did in preaching, and what I tried to do in this sermon, was more than simply to bring in mechanically the Old Testament background to a New Testament text. Ed was able to bring into the present a sense of the visceral reality of the Old Testament event so that we would hear, taste, and see the connections between treasures old and new. How many of us can forget Ed's description of David pouring out onto the dry ground the water his friends risked their lives to get from the well in Bethlehem (2 Sam. 23:13–17)?

Listening to Ed preach, we could always tell when he was about ready to bring home to us the power of the historic redemptive message: He would begin to rock back and forth as he would elevate his voice. He would begin almost to giggle as he saw us beginning to catch the connections and to elevate our own worship in that moment. And he would, as he did all this, worship himself.

The Lord's presence on the mountain of our worship was sometimes brought with quickening and healing force in Ed's words. No wonder that all of us who have made our contributions to this volume have attempted for ten or twenty or thirty years to do what Ed did when he preached. No wonder that I, for one, feel as if I come only to the outer edge of being able to do so. How foolish to try to "make it happen." Ed knew better; he was the most awe-filled person in the room when it would happen.

Ed told me he once preached at Schloss Mittersill, the retreat center in the Austrian Alps. He said that it was one of those times when the preacher finishes and there follows nothing but silence. No sound. No stirring. No hymn. No standing up to leave. Just silence. Just awe at the glory of the Savior. When Ed spoke of this, it never even occurred to him that such an account could reflect flatteringly on him as the preacher. He knew too well that awe of that kind only comes to the congregation and to the preacher by the palpable presence of glory.

In the hardest and darkest places in my own life, what I most need is not to be dazzled by the finesse of Ed's, or any preacher's, ability to draw the old into the new. Certainly I do not need a preacher attempting to imitate Ed. What I need is Jesus Christ. When my own sin, the complex weave of my personal history and raging will, worked so deeply into my own heart, as indeed it has in recent times, I most needed to see Jesus on the mountain of worship. We Protestants don't call it the beatific vision, but that's not a bad term for it. Only such soul-ravishing sightings will lift us out of our self-made infernos.

The purpose, design, and delivery of this sermon are intended to get at least the preacher, and perhaps some in the congregation, to the mountain.

The Scripture (Luke 9:28–36)[1]

> Now about eight days after these sayings he took with him Peter and John and James and went up on the mountain to pray. And as he was praying, the appearance of his face was altered, and his clothing became dazzling white. And behold, two men were talking with him, Moses and Elijah, who appeared in glory and spoke of his departure, which he was about to accomplish at Jerusalem. Now Peter and those who were with him were heavy with sleep, but when they became fully awake they saw his glory and the two men who stood with him. And as the men were parting from him, Peter said to Jesus, "Master, it is good that we are here. Let us make three tents, one for you and one for Moses and one for Elijah"—not knowing what he said. As he was saying these things, a cloud came and overshadowed them, and they were afraid as they entered the cloud. And a voice came out of the cloud, saying, "This is my Son, my Chosen One; listen to him!" And when the voice had spoken, Jesus was found alone. And they kept silent and told no one in those days anything of what they had seen.

The Sermon

It has been said that people worship at their work, that they work at their play, and that they play at their worship. Perhaps what we most need is to learn how to worship in our worship. Jonathan Edwards, who thought and wrote a lot about worship, apparently

---

1. Unless otherwise identified, Scripture citations in this sermon are from the ESV.

learned how to experience it, both personally and corporately. He said that in worship we should have soul-ravishing sightings of the beauty of the Lord. What in the world does that mean: soul-ravishing sightings? What kind of language is this? Should I see something in worship that I am not seeing? Should I realize something that I am not realizing? Should I experience things that I have not yet experienced? Edwards, who sometimes worshiped so intensely that he wept uncontrollably, would say the answer is yes. I am convinced that most of us are in the narthex or lobby of the house of worship, looking in but not sure we are ready to sing the first hymn, much less weep uncontrollably.

Yet, we are by nature worshipers. It is the way God made us; we are designed for worship. God has wired us in every way to worship. Preacher and author John Piper has told us that we are meant to enjoy that which we worship.[2] Wild and happy cheers on Friday night at high school football games remind us that we enjoy praising and exalting that which we love, that which is important to us. We praise what we love. If you think about it, the world is full of praise, isn't it?

We praise our team, we praise our girlfriends, or our wives, or our lovers. We praise our children or our grandchildren. We praise our political candidates. We praise the exceptional abilities of people. We praise Tiger Woods for his incredible accomplishments in his chosen field. Even our praise for our candidate or our favorite golfer is a hint to us that it is built into us to praise. When we love something, we exalt it; when we praise it, it feels so good that we know we were meant to do it. We were meant for exaltation, and ultimately we were meant for worship. This instinct to praise is really quite close to worship. The impulse to worship is because God made us for himself, for his worship. As St. Augustine famously said, "Our hearts are restless until they find their rest in Thee, O God."

In other words, all of our restless yearnings can actually be revealed in the praise and adoration that we give to so many things in our lives. We find ourselves giving our hearts away when we

2. John Piper, *Desiring God: Meditations of a Christian Hedonist* (Portland, OR: Multnomah, 1986), chapter 3, "Worship: The Feast of Christian Hedonism." The tenth anniversary (1996) expanded edition of *Desiring God* is also available online. Chapter 3 is at http://www.desiringgod.org/dg/id45.htm.

find ourselves invested, perhaps we could say overly invested, in many things, even good things. Actually, this should be a signal to us that we are made for something really splendid. We were made for something glorious. We were made to shine with the beauty of Christ. Now, I'm not even sure that I know what that means. But I think that there is a hint there of what we were made for. Don't you sense it sometimes? Maybe you have detected this hint during a morning worship service or while watching the sky go wildly red at sunset. You've sensed that something in your soul is rising. You've sensed something in your soul that is pure, something that is good. You've sensed the essence of the way God has made you and remade you and redeemed you in his Son, and all this rises up to say: "I need this. I want this. I need him. I want him. And yes, I can see a glimpse, just a glimpse. I want him more than anything. I want to hold on to this moment."

And then it goes away, doesn't it? It slides away and by the time the service is over, or shortly thereafter, your eyes and your mind and your heart are filled with many things, many good things—the need to get lunch, the need to plan for the meeting in the office on Monday morning or the Bible study that night, the need to get ready for your twelve-year-old's soccer practice or to write the grocery list. Good things . . . and sometimes things that are not so good. But where is that sighting that lifted your eyes and your heart, that soul-ravishing sighting that you had for just a moment or two? Oh, how you wish you could hold on to it!

As I have lived a life in which the "not so good" has threatened to overwhelm and undo the good, I have come to believe through Bible study and experience that the tragedy of sin and the fall is so deep in our hearts and our lives that we *must* worship. We must praise the One who will, by that worship, squeeze out the wrong in our hearts and the pain that wrong brings. Even so, the best we can frequently do is to get glimpses. But as we seek for those glimpses with all of our heart, the Lord promises that he will bring beauty to ugly places and show us the way to gaze at his perfect beauty. "One thing have I asked of the LORD," Psalm 27:4 says, "that will I seek after: that I may dwell in the house of the LORD all the days of my life, to gaze upon the beauty of the LORD and to inquire in his temple."

I want you to understand with me that private and corporate worship is the best, the most wonderful, the most glorious activity of our humanity. We were made for it. And I want you to understand with me that worship pushes out the smog caused by confusing the beauty of the Lord with anything else. As we worship, even with fits and starts and with restless hearts that want to *do something* for heaven's sake, the Lord, as a Man who understands our weakness and failings, comes down to us in our lostness, even the kind of lostness the Christian can know. He finds us here, here in this smoggy place called our lives, and he makes us want more and more of him, which leads to more and more worship.

Jesus "took with him Peter and John and James and went up on the mountain to pray." I wonder if you know why mountains are so important in the Bible. Maybe we think of mountains in the Bible as places where one goes to have "a mountain top experience," a spiritual high. Maybe mountains are where we metaphorically see that we are "on top of the world" as we are looking down. Maybe mountains are where we think we need to be in order to have a clearer perspective on life, to see a little bit of where our life is going.

All these may be true, but none of them are what mountains are about in the Bible. Rather, in the Bible, mountains are the places where beholding the Lord takes place, where men get glimpses of God and where men get glimpses of their own deepest identities. Mountains are places where God tells man about himself and where man finds out something about himself. Mountains are the place where God reveals himself so that people can begin to worship.

In Hebrews 12 it says that when we come to worship we actually come to a mountain. We are on a mountain in our worship services. The mountain to which we come is the new Mount Zion, as the author of Hebrews says, and we join together with the angels and the communion of saints from every generation. Somehow, in the wonderful mystery of worship, there are angels present. Also present are saints from every age, going back to the famous and the not so famous in every generation. They are all with us, or better yet, we are with them. We are with them on the mountain, the mountain where the holy temple is, Mount Zion. If you have been to Jerusalem, you know Mount Zion is a mountain—not a very big mountain, but it is a mountain. Now, the writer to the Hebrews says, the Mount Zion where we gather is not in Israel, not on earth at all, but is in "the heavenly Jerusalem." All of the songs of ascent in the Psalms, Psalms 120–134, are songs the people sang as they went up the mountain, to Mount Zion. For what purpose? To worship the Lord.

Mountains are where God revealed his wonder, his beauty, and his plan. You remember that God commanded Abraham to make a sacrifice of his son Isaac on *Mount* Moriah. Abraham took Isaac, the wood, and the knife and went up the mountain. God stopped him just in time and revealed himself in the provision of the sacrifice, the ram. On *Mount* Sinai God revealed himself to Moses and gave him the Law. You remember that Jesus, the greater Moses, gave the Law again in the Sermon on the *Mount*, on the *Mount* of Beatitudes. You remember that after the resurrection Jesus gave the charge to his disciples to go into all the world baptizing and teaching. But what you may have missed, perhaps, is that his charge was given on a *mountain* near Jerusalem. Do you remember what the disciples did even before Jesus spoke? It says they met him on the mountain he designated, and they worshiped him (Matt. 28:17). So even as the Lord gave to the church marching orders until he returns, these directions came in the context of worship on a mountain.

All places in Scripture where worship happens on a mountain are characterized by two realities. One is that *the presence of God is perceived*. Now let me suggest that "perceived" is a very nice and safe word. But really what happens is that the presence of God is felt, tasted, touched by the lives of people who dare to worship him there. The second thing that happens on mountains is that *God speaks*. When he speaks, his words become the revelation, the information that is needed in order to catch glimpses of who he is.

This is true here in Luke's Gospel, where we find this mountain on which God let himself be known and where he revealed his glory as he spoke to his disciples. Jesus took Peter, James, and John, and they went up to the mountain, and there his appearance was changed. It became radiant. His face was changed. His garments became glowingly white. In fact, the parallel passage in Mark's Gospel says that his clothes were whiter than any bleach could ever make them.

His being was filled with light. Can you imagine that? I think the words of Scripture invite us to imagine that. They invite us to think about what it must have looked and sounded like. For all intents and purposes, Jesus, to Peter, James, and John, was quite an ordinary looking man in his humanity. All of a sudden he was transfigured before their eyes so they saw him in a different way. His being was filled with light. Psalm 104:2 says that God wraps himself with light as with a garment. The word "wrap" is from an old Akkadian word that means to *darken*. In the psalm when it says that God wraps himself with light, it actually means he *darkens* himself with light. The psalmist is expressing poetically the apparent contradiction that God camouflages his being with that which we find revealing. In other words, God is so beautiful, he is so filled with splendid glory, that light actually hides it. You see, God is a God of glory. Glory is a word that means all of those things that we've been saying about God so far: that he is beautiful, that he's splendid, that he's majestic, that he's wonderful. All of the things that characterize God are summed up in this word "glory."

I wonder if you know what "glory" means in the language in which the Old Testament was originally written. It means "heavy." Weighty. It's almost like in the slang of the 1960s when people would say, "That's heavy, man." God is heavy, and he is weighty. He is the one thing that really matters. That is what Peter, James, and John began to understand in this passage. When they saw a revelation of the glory of the Son of God before their very eyes, they realized that in the end only one thing matters. Only one thing is weighty. Everything else is lightweight. So much of our lives is given to light-weight things. So much of our lives is given over to things that aren't weighty, aren't heavy, aren't important. We invest and over-invest in the amusements, the pleasures, and the accomplishments of this world, none of which are in and of themselves bad. But when they are isolated from the light and the weight of God, they become like feathers. And they don't matter at all.

John says: "We beheld his glory, the glory as of the only begotten ..." (John 1:14, KJV). That is what Peter, James, and John did. John said that in his Gospel. He ought to know because he was there. So later on when he writes about it, he says that what they saw on that mountain was his glory. In the same way Peter speaks of himself, James, and John as "eyewitnesses of his majesty" because they saw Jesus receive "honor and glory from God the Father . . ." as "we were with him on the holy mountain" (2 Pet. 1:16–18).

In his taking on flesh and identifying with us in all our need, Jesus abandoned his outward splendor, the splendor of the eternal Son of God that he had with the Father from all eternity. It says in Philippians 2 that he "emptied" himself. He emptied himself not of the *essence* of the eternal Son but of the *prerogatives* and *privileges* of being God's Son. He took off the outward splendor of his glory and laid it down in order to take up our flesh. Here now is a great wonder: since the time when Jesus took upon himself our flesh, he has never taken it off. Never. And he never will. Now in his resurrection, now as he sits at God's right hand waiting for us to come, now as he is there, all those who have gone to be with him see him as a man. But a splendid man, a glorious man, a man filled with light and glory, a man as you and I ought to be. Maybe one day we'll be something like that. You see what Peter, James, and John saw here was a taste of that future. They got a glimpse of it. And I dare say, it was a soul-ravishing glimpse.

What happened on the Mount of Transfiguration is very much like what happened in an earlier, Old Testament soul-ravishing sighting of God's glory. The story is told in Exodus 3:

> Now Moses was keeping the flock of his father-in-law, Jethro, the priest of Midian, and he led his flock to the west side of the wilderness and came to Horeb, the mountain of God. And the angel of the Lord appeared to him in a flame of fire out of the midst of a bush. He looked, and behold, the bush was burning, yet it was not consumed. And Moses said, "I will turn aside to see this great sight, why the bush is not burned." When the Lord saw that he turned aside to see, God called to him out of the bush, "Moses, Moses!" And he said, "Here I am." Then he said, "Do not come near; take your sandals off your feet, for the place on which you are standing is holy ground." And he said, "I am the God of your father, the God of Abraham, the

God of Isaac, and the God of Jacob." And Moses hid his face, for he was afraid to look at God. (Ex. 3:1–6)

Moses was on the desert's backside, tending after his father-in-law's sheep, a job that surely must have bored him. He wandered to Horeb, called the mountain of God, and there his boredom came swiftly to an end. On the mountain, there was a bush; it was burning, but was evidently made of some kind of renewable or indestructible matter that was not burned up. No ashes. Just fire. Moses went closer—he "turned aside"—to the bush that was burning but not consumed. I can almost hear Moses saying something like: "Why, God is here in this marvelous thing! Isn't this wonderful; isn't this interesting? Let's get together and have a meeting, have a program, maybe talk about this a little bit. This is very interesting."

In verse 2 it says that Moses "looked." I want to tell you that the word" looked" does not mean simply to see, or to catch a glimpse. Even less does it mean to behold the beauty of the Lord. The word means to look in such a way in order to comprehend and to control. What Moses was trying to do was to get this "great sight" under his control. It was as if Moses were saying, "Thank you very much for this most interesting revelation. I need to figure this out. Now would you tell me a little more about what this means?"

This is so similar to what Peter does on the Mount of Transfiguration. "Isn't this wonderful, isn't this interesting? Let's get together and discuss this further; perhaps form a committee to look into this. This is very interesting. I've got to figure this out. This is very interesting, God. Thank you very much for this little revelation. Now would you tell me a little bit more about what this means?"

Then out of the bush came a voice, just like the voice that came out of the cloud on the Mount of Transfiguration. The voice said, "Moses, Moses." (The repetition of a name is always God's way of saying, "I know you. I know all about you, your quirks, your oddities, your need, your sin . . . Martha, Martha. Peter, Peter. Susie, Susie. Hank, Hank.") "This is my Son. Be quiet. Take your sandals off. The ground is holy."

And then we read that Moses did the right thing, the logical thing: he hid his face from God. And it says in Matthew's account of the

Transfiguration that when the disciples realized who they were dealing with, they too fell down on their faces, and they hid their faces
from God. It's logical.

But you know, they did something else, too. They did something
else before they did that. It's very interesting that what they tried to
do is just what Moses tried to do on the mountain top. Peter came
along and he said something like, "This is really swell up here. Lord,
good to see you. Moses is here, Elijah is here too. My gracious, what a
party. Glad you guys showed up for our meeting. You ought to stick
around for a while. You know, I'll build a little tabernacle."

We don't know why Peter said that. Maybe it had something to
do with trying to control this thing, just like Moses had done when
he tried to control the phenomenon of the burning bush with his
gaze. You know, our first task as Christians is not to figure God out.
It's not even to be useful to God. It is rather to be awe-full, to be full
of awe. It is to simply understand that this is a God from whom we
should rightly hide our faces. This God is so full of splendid holiness
and glory that no man can stand before him. That is what we must
learn first. God silences our attempts at religion. Again and again:
"Moses! Moses! Take your sandals off." And then to Peter: "This is
my beloved Son. Listen to him!" In other words: "Stop talking and
start listening."

You must see that there is a tension here in both of these accounts.
On the one hand, of course, God draws close to us in Jesus and he
is near to us. This is the whole meaning of the incarnation, the in-
fleshment of Jesus. It is the meaning, too, of the indwelling Spirit:
I am with you. The term used to describe this closeness of God is
"immanent." God is immanent. He is also transcendent. He is other.
There is a certain sense in which these disciples, just like Moses,
and just like us, needed to learn that we can't be so familiar with
Jesus. Like us, Peter, James, and John thought that Jesus was their
buddy, their friend. They had been with him for three years. They
had identified with him, and he with them. But they were startled
on the mountain when they got a fuller picture of who he was. "We
didn't know!" What an awful thing it would be if one day we find
ourselves standing before the Lord in all of his glory, and we look at
him and we have to say, "I didn't know. I didn't get it."

But he is different. There is a closeness that he has with the Father that we can't understand. In fact at one point he says, "I am ascending to my Father and your Father . . ." (John 20:17). He cannot even say that he ascends to *our Father* because whatever his relationship is to the Father, it is different from our relationship to the Father. There is awesomeness and strangeness to him. He leaves the crowd for solitude at the most unexpected times.

Most of all, what makes him different is that he must go where they cannot go. "Where I am going, you cannot follow." It is in his *leaving*, in his departure, it is when Jesus gets ready to leave, that he is so very different from anything that any of us will ever be. It is his departure in Jerusalem via the cross that sets him utterly apart from us forever. Luke says that Jesus was talking to Moses and Elijah about his departure that he was about to accomplish in Jerusalem. That is why Moses and Elijah were there. Jesus was having a conversation in Hebrew or Aramaic with two people who just happened to be *experts in departures*. Remember Elijah's departure in 2 Kings when he went up to God in a chariot of fire? That was a fairly dramatic departure, don't you agree? But it was Moses who was the real expert in departures. The manner of his departure was very dramatic, wasn't it? It's fair to say that two million men, women, and children left Egypt with Egyptian clothing, Egyptian livestock, Egyptian food, Egyptian silver and gold, and the Egyptians' blessing. When the Egyptians realized that the Israelites were getting away with too much, they went after them. And when they went after them, Moses took the rod that God had given to him and held it out over the water, and the water separated, and the people of Israel went through. When the Egyptians followed them, the water covered them up and drowned them. That is fairly dramatic!

But if the *manner* of Moses' departure was dramatic, then the *meaning* of it was even more dramatic. When God delivered his people from Egypt, he delivered them out of the bondage of sin and into the hope of the Promised Land. The meaning of Moses' departure is that it spoke of Christ who would free us from the slavery to sin and give us the liberty of being sons of God. What does a son of God have the right to do? He has a right to come into his Father's presence and to gaze upon his Father. Not with a gaze that seeks to control, but a gaze that worships. That is just what we do in worship! Peter, James, and John saw the glory of God's Son revealed on the mountain as the One who has all glory and all power, who was ready to make the most important departure in all of human history. Worship is compelled by a vision of who God really is in his Son. There is no other way to learn to worship except to look and gaze upon the face of Christ. Peter, James, and John had the same instinctive reaction that Moses did. They hid their faces. They were right. Moses was right. But together with Moses, Peter, James, and John, we can know God's soul-ravishing glory, as the apostle Paul puts it: "For God, who said, 'Let light shine out of darkness,' has shone in our hearts to give the light of the knowledge of the glory of God in the face of Jesus Christ" (2 Cor. 4:6). Where do you see the glory of God? In the face of Jesus.

Here is my plea to you. Seek his face. My plea to you is to seek him with all your heart. Or as the psalmist puts it in Psalm 63:

> O God, you are my God; earnestly I seek you;
>   my soul thirsts for you;
> my flesh faints for you,
>   as in a dry and weary land where there is no water.
> So I have looked upon you in the sanctuary,
>   beholding your power and glory. (Ps. 63:1–2)

I love beautiful churches with beautiful sanctuaries. I believe they are "incarnational" reminders of the beauty of the Lord. But the sanctuary where we look upon God and see his power and glory is not a building. It is people, the people of God in worship. We are the sanctuary when we come together. God promises. That is his Word. What I just read to you in Psalm 63 is his Word. God stakes everything on his Word. In his Word he promises he will reveal himself in soul-ravishing sightings in his sanctuary when his people are together.

Certainly you should worship in your private time with the Lord. But come to worship *together* in this place. Come and expect God to ravish your soul. Seek it. Seek him. Don't be content with clock-punching worship in your private worship time: "Okay, there it is, my fifteen minutes! Did it. Bam. Good. Got that checked off today."

Don't let go of God until he finds you. Hold onto him without the presumption that Peter had when he sought to hang onto Jesus, Moses, and Elijah on top of the mountain. Without presumption, but rather with expectation, we lift our faces up. Moses hid his face. Peter, James, and John hid their faces. But now you and I have a greater privilege than any of them. We are bid to lift up our faces in worship and to look, to behold Jesus Christ in all of his beauty.

Some of you are brand new to all of this. Some of you are saying, "I don't know what it is to seek or to see Jesus at all." For you, the promise is that if you will seek him in worship, he will find you. If you seek him, you will find yourself being found. You will find this wonderful gospel of his departure and you will understand that he left via the cross for you. He came for you and died for you. He gave everything for you. He lived the life for you that you could not live, and he died the death you could not die. He gives that life to you now as a gift that you are to take freely by his grace without merit of your own. Simply say, "Thank you."

After forty years of stumbling up mountains after Jesus, I'm only really beginning to learn what to do and what not to do on those mountains. Too many other things clouded my sight and kept me from gazing on the one beautiful thing that matters. Too many ideas, too many programs, too many people to please. I went into many worship spaces, but too few sanctuaries. I organized choirs and ushers and sermons and organs. I planned many worship services and saw how to make it all happen in sixty-five minutes. But I didn't see Jesus. Now, I am beginning to worship. Now I want to see Jesus come down; to see Jesus teaching and loving and healing and praying; to see Jesus take bread and break it; to see Jesus stagger to the cross; to see Jesus with wounds bless his confused followers; to see Jesus lifted up to glory . . . Glory! . . . Beauty! Now what I want is to see just glimpses . . . soul-ravishing sightings. Gazing at him, I am changed . . . transformed from one sighting of glory to another . . . soul-ravishing.

11

THE GREATNESS OF GOD'S ULTIMATE WORD

Hebrews 1:1–3

Arturo G. Azurdia III

Introduction

On the one hand, I have no business contributing to this collection of sermons in honor of Edmund P. Clowney. I state this, however, not in self-induced modesty, but as an accurate assessment of my gifts and abilities when set in contrast to his. Surely one of the greatest blessings granted a seminary student is the privilege of being overwhelmed by a professor who, in genuine humility and meekness, possesses a vast erudition and seemingly limitless knowledge of the sacred text. Such a professor becomes something of a hero, a mentor, a theological father. To this day, it is Dr. Clowney who occupies this unique place in my life and affections. I will forever be his student as even now, when I read (and re-read) his work, I am mindful of a vast, pious scholarship that unmistakably

dwarfs my own and yet simultaneously compels me to greater discipline and diligence when seeking to comprehend the relationship
of a single biblical text to the Bible's overarching theme: God's
purpose to redeem the human race through his Son, Jesus Christ.

On the other hand, to decline the invitation to contribute to this
volume would undoubtedly leave me with a sense of wistful disappointment. Not merely because my experience as a student of Dr.
Clowney's was uniquely intellectual, but because it so unexpectedly
and radically altered the trajectory of my life and ministry.

Preaching Christ from the Old Testament was the name of the
class. I entered it with my resistance level at its peak because years
earlier I had been outfitted with a hermeneutic that argued one
must never preach Christ unless he is mentioned in the specific text
at hand. Of course, the negative corollary was equally emphatic:
preaching Christ from the entire Bible could only be the result of
medieval allegorizing—a Bible study approach to be spurned as an
interpretive interloper. Yet for three hours each day Dr. Clowney
displayed from both exegetical and theological perspectives how
the Old Testament relentlessly points to Jesus Christ. At the risk of
sounding hopelessly sentimental, it was something of an Emmaus
Road experience for me. Each day my heart burned, aroused by two
conflicting emotions: (1) fresh affection (for the glory and greatness
of my Savior) and (2) intensifying frustration. At the conclusion of
the third class session I approached Dr. Clowney and declared, "I
can't preach Jesus Christ if he is not in the text." Very matter-of-
factly he responded, "Oh, yes, you can." So I repeated myself more
emphatically, "Dr. Clowney, I can't preach Jesus if he is not *specifically* mentioned in the text." "Oh, yes, you can," he replied graciously,
contrary to my tone. Then, amazingly (arrogantly?), I asserted myself
a third time with little attempt to mask my frustration, *"I can't
preach Jesus if he isn't in the text!"*

I will never forget Dr. Clowney's response. He smiled, gently
put his hand on my shoulder, and said, "You don't know your Bible
well enough." Though I had earned the equivalent of two Master's
degrees in Bible and theology and had been engaged in pastoral
ministry for more than a decade, he was exactly right. As an experienced theological physician he accurately diagnosed my internal

conflict by the obvious, external symptoms. It proved to be one of the most meaningful experiences in my entire Christian pilgrimage, and certainly the most significant moment in my theological development. I finished the class with a resolve to spend the rest of my life learning how to preach Christ from the entire Bible—a resolve that subsequently marked my efforts as a pastor and now shapes my role as a professor assigned the task of teaching seminarians preparing for expository ministry. I rarely speak without the distinct influence of Dr. Clowney expressing itself in my words.

The following sermon was preached in 2006 to a historic congregation in Portland, Oregon—historic in the sense that: (1) its existence spans well over a hundred years; and (2) it displays a legacy of significant gospel influence that has reached around the world. This congregation is largely, though not exclusively, comprised of senior adults who have been Christians for many years. Their life together has been irrefutably distinguished by a long-term fidelity to the Bible.

Why, then, did I choose to preach Hebrews 1:1–3? In a very real sense, the ethos of this congregation mirrors what had been my own inadequate commitment from earlier days: a resolute devotion to the Scriptures without appreciating the abiding influence of its meta-narrative. Hence, while the gospel's value is certainly regarded as indispensable to the inception of the Christian life, it appears to be *assumed* with regard to the ongoing perseverance of people who are already Christians. Of course, this assumption would never be espoused. Rather, the fine Christians of this faithful congregation would flatly reject such a notion. Nevertheless, as is the case with so many Bible-believing congregations, the deficiency exists not in the promulgation of heterodoxy, but in their lack of preoccupation with their most essential message.

My earliest recollection of Dr. Clowney's instruction is his assertion that Jesus of Nazareth is established as the ultimate fulfillment of the three Old Testament offices: prophet, priest, and king. Of course, while this is made plainly evident throughout the entire New Testament corpus, it proves to be a predominant stream of instruction in the sermon to the Hebrews.[1] In fact, it emerges almost immediately in the sermon's introduction.

For example, God's Son is the great *priest* who actually accomplishes what every prior priest could only foreshadow: he effects a once-and-for-all-time "purification for sins" (Heb. 1:3). And how was the completion of his purifying work authenticated? This priest "sat down"—an act withheld from all preceding priests, as indicated by the conspicuous absence of any place to sit inside the temple (Heb. 10:11–12). His sitting down, however, was not for the purpose of catching his breath after his laborious work of redemption. It was an act of enthronement, as he was seated "at the right hand of the Majesty on high." In the ancient world this was regarded as the place of unparalleled glory and sovereignty. Jesus Christ, the sermon asserts, is the great *king*. Finally, he is the great *prophet*—the One by whom God "in these last days . . . has spoken to us" (Heb. 1:2)—a prophet far superior to all the earlier prophets sent by God because he is God's very Son.

Karl Barth was once asked if he did not agree that God had revealed himself in many religions besides Christianity. "No," he answered (in typical Barthian fashion), "God has not revealed himself in any religion, *including* Christianity. He has spoken in his Son, Jesus Christ."[2]

I didn't learn this from Barth. I learned it from Edmund Clowney, a theological mentor to whom I will forever acknowledge indebtedness for teaching me to read the Bible not as an inspired book of virtues but as a "him" book—a book that, from cover to cover, designedly points me to Jesus Christ, God's ultimate Word.

The Scripture (Hebrews 1:1–3)[3]

Long ago God spoke to the fathers by the prophets at different times and in different ways. In these last days, He has spoken to us by [His] Son, whom He has appointed heir of all things and through

---

1. William L. Lane, *Hebrews 1–8*, Word Biblical Commentary 47A (Waco: Word, 1991), lxx–lxxv.

2. Cited in Leighton Ford, "Is It Still Gospel Preaching?" *Leadership* 29.1 (Winter 2008): 27–30. Barth further develops this concept in *Church Dogmatics*, vol. 1.2 *The Doctrine of the Word of God* (London: T&T Clark, 2004).

3. Unless otherwise indicated, Scripture citations in this sermon are from the HCSB.

whom He made the universe. He is the radiance of His glory, the exact expression of His nature, and He sustains all things by His powerful word. After making purification for sins, He sat down at the right hand of the Majesty on high.

The Sermon

Have you ever felt that God was silent at the very moment you most needed him to speak? That you really wanted him to speak— that you desperately needed him to speak—but that all you heard from him was the deafening sound of silence? When the pathologist tells you: "The tumor is malignant" . . . When your ob-gyn says: "The baby you're carrying has Down syndrome" . . . When you discover that your spouse has been unfaithful . . . or that you've been laid off . . . or that your teenager has been hit by a drunk driver? You come to God, laying bare your heart, and you cry out for explanation, *"Why?"* But all you get in response is *silence*. Have you ever felt that God was silent at the very moment you most needed him to speak?

Jesus Christ knew that very same experience when, on the cross, he cried out for explanation: "My God, My God, *why* have you forsaken me?" What was the response of his Father? There was no response. No explanation. There was only silence. Absolute silence. Inescapable silence. But *forever* silence? No! We are here this morning because three days later his Father spoke. And his response came loudly and clearly when he raised his Son, Jesus, from the dead.

You see, friends, the crucifixion and resurrection of Jesus Christ tell us that God's silence is never the silence of indifference, never the silence of a lack of compassion. Rather, God's silence is always an eloquent silence—a silence that sets the stage for his eventual, and most powerful, speaking. It is this, now, that brings us to the meaning of the opening paragraph in this inspired sermon that has come to us as the letter to the Hebrews.

It was written to a small group of Jewish Christians living in Rome—people who had first heard the gospel preached by those who had been eyewitnesses of Jesus Christ. By the grace of God, they had emerged from Judaism's shadows into the fully-flowered substance of Christian faith. But all of this at no small cost, you must understand. While Rome appeared somewhat ambivalent toward people of Jewish descent, its feelings for Christianity were very clearly defined: Rome detested all things Christian. As such, these Christians had endured suffering, ridicule, imprisonment, and the confiscation of their possessions. Now, with a psychotic leader named Nero on the throne—and hungry lions eager to be released into the arena of the Coliseum—these Jewish Christians connect the dots: their allegiance to Jesus Christ may very well be put to the ultimate test.

And so, just like you and me, they begin to ask the hard questions: "Where is God in this? Doesn't he know what's going on? Has he lost sight of us? Doesn't he care? Why is he allowing this to take place?" As God seems to stay silent, these unanswered questions evoke the consideration of a possibility: "*Maybe we ought to go back to Judaism.* It's not as if we'd be embracing the Roman pantheon of gods. After all, Judaism is close to Christianity, isn't it? And, most of all, it's safe. So what do you think? Should we step back into the synagogue? What viable alternative are we left with, given God's apparent silence?"

But then a whisper is passed through the underground: "A word has arrived." At the appointed time—most likely in the privacy of a home—the frightened congregation gathers. A man stands to his feet, unrolls the parchment, and begins to read aloud: "Long ago God spoke to the fathers by the prophets at different times and in different ways. In these last days, He has spoken to us by [His] Son . . ." (Heb. 1:1–2). An immediate realization dawns on the minds of those who hear these words read for the first time: "What have we been thinking? Maybe it was a momentary brain lapse, but we can't go back to Judaism."

But some of you are saying, "Now you've lost me. I'm not getting your point. Why do these opening words imply that these Jewish Christians cannot go back to Judaism?"

Did you catch the series of contrasts that distinguish verse 1 from verse 2? To begin with, take note of the contrast in the *timing* of God's communication: "long ago" (v. 1) over against "in these last days" (v. 2). It's a distinction between *then* and *now*. Secondly, notice the contrast in the *recipients* of God's communication: God spoke "to the fathers" (v. 1) over against his speaking "to us" (v. 2). It's a distinction between *them* and *us*. The most striking contrast, however, is with regard to the *instruments* of God's communication: "God spoke . . . by the prophets" (v. 1), a reference easy enough to understand: those wonderful men and women of faith who served as God's spokespersons during in the Old Testament epoch. But now, they are set over against a *qualitatively* different spokesperson: "In these last days, He (God) has spoken to us by [His] Son" (v. 2). Actually, to be quite literal, the text reads: "God has spoken to us by Son." Not "by the Son," or "by his Son." Simply: "*by Son.*" This construction draws our attention to the unique *nature* of this One in whom God has spoken. In other words, over against the prophets, God has now spoken to us by means of One who possesses the distinct quality of being his own Son.

Do you feel the weight of these distinctions? *Now*—as opposed to then? *To us*—over against them? *By his Son*—instead of the prophets? To the original listeners the only possible response would be obvious: "How could we ever go back to Judaism? To do so would represent a colossal leap in the wrong direction."

Do you recall the scene that occurred on the Mount of Transfiguration? Before three of his disciples, Jesus is overpoweringly manifested in an exhibition of his resplendent glory. But Jesus is not alone. Appearing with him are Moses and Elijah. What is Peter's response to this revelation? "Lord, it's good for us to be here! If You want, I will make three tabernacles here: one for You, one for Moses, and one for Elijah" (Matt. 17:4). Peter quickly connects the theological dots—so he thinks—and his assumption is: "Here is Moses—the giver of the Law. Here is Elijah—the premier representative of the prophetic order. And here is our Jesus—the newest spokesman in a club comprising the great revealers of divine truth." But how does God disabuse (or "cure") Peter of his heresy? "*This* is My beloved Son. . . . Listen to *Him!*" (Matt. 17:5). "This One is infinitely more than the latest in a line-up of famous prophetic speakers. He is of an altogether different kind. *He* is my *Son. Listen* to *him.*"

Of course, God is not suggesting that the Old Testament is now irrelevant to us; rather, a progression has been made in the Bible's storyline—a forward movement from promise to fulfillment, from shadow to substance, from prophet to Prophet *par excellence*, all of which implies that Judaism can no longer be an acceptable alternative. How, for example, could a Christian ever return to the animal sacrifices knowing that the ultimate Lamb of God has been slain? Judaism will no longer do. Thus, interspersed throughout this book are several of the strongest warnings found anywhere in the Bible. At the heart of each of them is this straightforward plea: "You mustn't go back. You mustn't turn away. You've come out of the shadows and into the light. Don't step back into the darkness." And why not? "Because God's Son is *better.*" It's the repeated theme permeating the entire sermon to the Hebrews: God's Son is better—better than the prophets, better than Moses, better than Joshua, better than the priests, better than the animal sacrifices, better than the old covenant. He is better than *everything* and *everyone.*

Now, you've been very patient as I've sought to establish something of an original setting for this sermon to Hebrew Christians long ago and far away. Allow me, however, to become much more personal at this point. Is it possible that you've been tempted in a way analogous to these Hebrew Christians—that is, to return to your former manner of life because doing so would seem to make your situation so much easier to endure? Of course, my expectation is that Judaism *per se* poses no allurement away from Jesus Christ— at least not for most of you. But that's not to say that nothing else does. Maybe the siren song calling you away from Jesus Christ is a lifestyle of pleasing your appetites—a lifestyle given over to the reckless pursuit of sexual excitement . . . or financial prosperity . . . or professional success.

Are you a high school student? If you were not a Christian you could readily cheat on an exam to earn a scholarship, steal from your parents to buy a new IPod, or shoot up steroids to enhance your athletic performance. And you could do all of it without the slightest twinge of unrest in your conscience—if you were not a Christian.

Are you negotiating with yourself these days? Wrestling with these kinds of temptations? Not altogether sure what choices you'll make tomorrow? Reminiscing about the "easier days" of your pre-Christian life? You must not walk away from Jesus Christ. To do so could prove eternally catastrophic.

"But you don't know what I have to live with," you retort. "It's no convenience for me to be a Christian. To the contrary, it costs me nearly every day of my life. How do you expect me to persevere through the inescapable hardships that relentlessly haunt me as a consequence of identifying myself as a follower of Jesus Christ?"

The answer, my friend, is that you persevere by submitting yourself to a reinvigorating vision of the Son of God. As a consequence, you'll discover that you cannot turn away from him, that you will not turn away from him—that his greatness is too compelling, his majesty too alluring, his glory too captivating. Rather than forsake him, you would willingly surrender everything to have him.

It's the very thing the preacher to the Hebrews is saying here: God's last days' Word has come to us. But not this time on cold, hard, unbending tablets of stone; rather, in a living, breathing human being—his very Son. But this raises a question: What is it about him that is compelling enough to keep Christians from going back to *anything* or *anyone* else? What is it, in particular, that distinguishes his all-surpassing greatness? Let me set before you three summary statements that establish the unequaled greatness of this last days' Word from God.

He Is the Cosmic Lord

God's Son—this ultimate Word from God—is the beginning and the ending of everything. He is the One who calls everything into existence. He is the One who carries everything forward to its appointed destiny. And he is the One in whom everything culminates.

Watch how this all comes together: "In these last days, he has spoken to us by his Son, whom he appointed heir of all things" (we'll come back to this), *"and through whom He made the universe"* (1:2). For all of *our* intellectual prowess and technological ability, humanity still cannot even create a particle of dust out of nothing. By contrast this Son spoke and, by virtue of a word that was instantaneously performative, the entire universe obediently sprang into existence. Have you ever considered what this means? The Cambridge physicist Stephen Hawking tells us (in *A Brief History of Time*[4]) that our galaxy is more than one hundred thousand light-years in diameter. What is a *light-year*? The distance that light can travel in one year. How fast does light travel? Pretty fast: 186,000 miles per second. If we multiply that by a year of seconds we are confronted with a galaxy possessing a diameter of about 600 trillion miles. Moreover, Hawking asserts that our galaxy is only one of a hundred thousand million galaxies!

Does this unnerve you? I hope not. It should expand your faith rather than undermine it. Why? This Son, by whom God has spoken to us in these last days, is the creator of everything. The Gospel of John says it like this: "In the beginning was the Word, and the Word was with God, and the Word was God. . . . All things were created through Him, and apart from Him not one thing was created that has been created" (John 1:1–3).

But the cosmic Lordship of God's Son extends beyond the mere *creation* of all things. It manifests itself in his *sustaining* of all things: He is "the radiance of his glory" (we'll come back to this), "the exact expression of His nature" (we'll come back to this), *"and He sustains all things by His powerful word"* (1:3). This Son is not an uninvolved deity—a hands-off god who sets the created universe in motion only then to ignore it in passive disengagement. This Son is intimately engaged with his creation.

I'm told that our sun has a surface temperature of twelve thousand degrees Fahrenheit. If the earth were any closer to the sun, we would burn up; or if any further away, we would freeze. Our globe, I'm told, is tilted on an exact angle of twenty-three degrees, providing us with four seasons. If it were not so tilted, vapors from the oceans would move north and south and develop into monstrous continents of ice. I'm told that if the moon did not retain its exact distance from the earth, the tides of the ocean would inundate the land completely—twice a day. That if the ocean floors were merely a few feet deeper than they are, the carbon dioxide and oxygen balance of the earth's atmosphere would be altogether upset, so that no animal or plant life could exist. So how does our universe exist

4. Stephen Hawking, *A Brief History of Time: From the Big Bang to Black Holes* (New York: Bantam, 1988).

in this incredibly delicate balance? The text answers: the Son of God "sustains all things." But we're not to imagine him in a way analogous to the Greek god Atlas who bears the weight of the world on his shoulders. The idea conveyed here is something more dynamic; it includes movement—the idea of carrying something forward to its appointed end.

Anne of Green Gables is a warm-hearted film about an orphan who, seemingly by accident, finds herself in the care of an elderly sister and brother, Marilla and Matthew. As the narrative unwinds, little Anne matures into young womanhood and, in so doing, worms her way deeply into their affections. When the day arrives for Anne to depart for college, she boards a train for her long journey. As the train pulls out of the station, a tender and telling conversation ensues between Marilla and Matthew:

> Marilla: I'm afraid for her, Matthew. She'll be gone so long. She'll get terrible lonesome.
> Matthew: You mean we'll get terrible lonesome.
> Marilla: I can't help wishing that she'd stayed a little girl.
> Matthew: Mrs. Spencer made a lucky mistake, I guess.
> Marilla: It wasn't luck. It was Providence. He knew we needed her.[5]

It's the very idea being conveyed here in Hebrews. Not only did this Son of God *create* everything, he providentially *guides* that everything to its intended destiny. But how does he accomplish this? "He sustains all things *by his powerful word*." Do you realize what this implies? No stress for the Son of God. No burden. No sleepless nights. No second-guessing. No wringing of the hands. No ulcers. No effort. He executes his providential purpose simply: by the sheer power of his word.

But not only does this Son *create* all things and *sustain* all things. As God's Son he *inherits* all things. Of course, this makes perfect sense, doesn't it? He is the *Son*—God's *only* Son. Sons inherit, don't they? And such is the case with *this* Son: he inherits everything.

5. *Anne of Green Gables* (Canadian Broadcasting Corporation, 1985; Kevin Sullivan, director; Kevin Sullivan and Joe Wiesenfeld, screenwriters).

But notice, now, what I previously overlooked regarding him: He has been *"appointed heir of all things . . ."* (1:2). He has become the heir of everything by *divine appointment*—which means that this expression, "heir of all things," is more than just a statement of fact. It's a *title* of dignity.

Some time ago I was preaching at a conference outside of London. Following one of the meetings I was introduced to a man named Fred Catherwood—or, as I was later informed, *Sir* Fred Catherwood. He'd been knighted by the Queen, appointed that title by virtue of his extraordinary service to the British Empire. And here in the text of Hebrews, this title given to God's Son shares much of the same idea. By virtue of his coming to us, purchasing our salvation by means of his death on the cross in our place, God raised his Son from the dead. In turn, he ascended into heaven where he has been appointed "heir of all things." It is a title that identifies his unequaled greatness—his supreme place over the entire universe—the consummate fulfillment of Psalm 2 where God says to his kingly Son: "Ask of Me, and I will make the nations Your inheritance, and the ends of the earth Your possession" (Ps. 2:8). Here, however, this divine inheritance extends beyond the boundaries of earth and becomes cosmic in proportion.

All of this means that everything that has ever been created has been created *for* the Son of God. The solar systems have been created *for him*. The angelic realms have been created *for him*. This planet and every single person on it—including you—have been created *for him*. Everything that has ever been made, from the largest galaxy to the tiniest microbe, has been made *for his pleasure and glory*. And I can assure you, nothing will escape his heirship—not one rebellious angel, not one rebellious human being, not one rebellious atom. It reveals his unequaled greatness, doesn't it? Can this be said of anyone else—that he is the creator, the sustainer, the inheritor of everything? The Son of God—the ultimate Word from God—he is the cosmic Lord.

He Is the Incarnate God

Look at what the preacher now says of God's Son: "He is the radiance of His [God's] glory, the exact expression of His nature . . ."

(v. 3). Now, my friends, we have to be very careful with these two statements because, in a very real sense, the *glory* of *deity* is not so much to be explained as it is to be adored. The Old Testament, however, can be of significant help to us at this point.

Let me ask you: "Where, in the Hebrew Scriptures was the radiance of God's glory seen—the visible glory of God?"

"Well," you say, "the visible glory of God was seen by Moses in the burning bush." Exactly.

"It also appeared at the giving of the Law on Mount Sinai. It then came upon the Tabernacle in the wilderness, and later the temple in Jerusalem." Right at every point.

But its *primary* location became a place within that temple called "the Holy of Holies." What was inside the Holy of Holies? The ark of the covenant. What rested on the top of that ark? The mercy seat. Positioned on both sides of the mercy seat? The mighty cherubim—angels uniquely associated with the very presence of God. And in that place—above the mercy seat, between the cherubim—was the visible manifestation of the glory of God. It was the most holy place on this planet.

But what does the Old Testament record eventually tell us about this glory? The prophet Ezekiel witnesses its abandonment of the temple, so that idolatrous Israel is left a sanctuary without the glory. The Jerusalem temple becomes a God-forsaken shell. Nevertheless, Ezekiel's prophecy ends with a great reversal: the promise of the Glory returning to a great last days' temple.

How astounding, then, are the opening words to John's Gospel, which tell us that the eternal Word—the divine Word—"became flesh and *tabernacled* among us. We observed his *glory*" (John 1:14, AGA[6]). Moreover, what does Jesus himself say in the very next chapter? "Destroy this temple, and I will raise it up in three days" (John 2:19, AGA). The apostle himself then adds his own, helpful commentary: "But he was speaking about the *temple* of his body" (2:21, AGA). Do you see what John is saying? His meaning would prove unmistakable to any Jewish reader of his Gospel: in the transformation of fulfillment, Christ is himself the last days' temple, the dwell-

---

6. Scripture quotations marked AGA indicate Arturo Azurdia's translation, modifying the wording of the HCSB.

ing of God with humanity. In other words, the glory *has* returned
and its locus is in Jesus Christ. Or to state it as our ancient preacher
to the Hebrews does: this Son is *"the radiance* (the outraying) *of
God's glory."*

Moreover, he adds: *"the exact expression of his nature."* In the ancient
world, a business transaction was consummated by the drafting of
a legal document representing the terms of the agreement. Instead
of signing one's name on a line at the bottom, however, a merchant
would place a dab of warm wax on the parchment, into which he
would then impress the image of his personal stamp. What remains
when he lifts his stamp from the document? An image in the wax
that is an "exact expression" of the image on his personal stamp.

This is the very idea being employed here with reference to this
Son by whom God now speaks to us. It means, for all practical purposes, that no one can ever legitimately say, "Well, I love God, but I
want no relationship with this Son." The refusal of the Son is nothing
less than the rejection of God himself. This Son, after all, is not the
chief angel. He is not the greatest of all created beings. He is not an
unusually gifted spiritual guide. He is the eternal God who has come
to us in the fullness of humanity. His compelling greatness, then, is
unequaled. He is the cosmic Lord and the incarnate God.

He Is the Priestly King

Continuing the description of this Son, the preacher adds: "After
making purification for sins, He sat down . . ." (1:3).

Sin does many devastating things to us, dear friends, far more
than we could ever fully understand. But among the most graphic of
these is that sin defiles us. It stains us. In the eyes of God it makes us
filthier than a dirty stable. And, of course, the problem at this point
is that everything about God is clean. Not the slightest impurity is
allowable in his presence—all of which exposes our glaring need for
purification. But how do we get clean? I can't clean you . . . and you
can't clean me. Two kids in a mud puddle can't clean each other up.
So how do we get clean?

Have you ever read the book of Leviticus? Dirty people are made
clean by means of priests offering sacrifices. In fact, on one day each
year the high priest would enter the Holy of Holies and sprinkle

blood on the mercy seat that I described earlier. It brought about a kind of temporary cleansing, but it really didn't get the job done—as evidenced by the fact that the priests' work never ended. They offered sacrifices *ad infinitum*—year after year, decade after decade, century after century.

By the way—as an interesting side note—have you ever considered the furniture inside the temple—the furnishings prescribed by God himself? He was very emphatic to Moses: "Make it just the way I tell you." And so, inside the Holy of Holies there was only the ark of the covenant. Just outside the Holy of Holies was a room called the Holy Place in which there was the altar of incense, the table for the showbread, a six-branched lampstand (for the tabernacle; later, ten lampstands for the temple), and two decorative pillars with bowls and chains (Exodus 25; 37; 1 Kings 7:15–50).

Have you ever considered the amount of work that occurred inside the temple? The priests were very busy, offering morning and evening sacrifices every single day. It seems to me, given the incessant activity, that an essential piece of furniture is missing from that place—an accouterment conspicuous by its absence. Was this something that God overlooked, perhaps, in his interior decorating? *There's nothing on which to sit down.* There's no provision of a place to sit. Not a chair. Not a bench. Not even so much as a stool! Why the *apparent* oversight? *Because it was never appropriate for a priest to sit down.* Why not? Because his work of making purification was never done. All of his offerings and efforts couldn't cleanse one person of any single sin. So why engage in all the ritual?

Because of what it foreshadowed: the coming of this *Son.* And when *he* was sacrificed—*he* who is the radiance of God's glory and the exact expression of his nature—*he* declared from the cross a statement that had never before been uttered by a priest: "It is finished!" And then what happened? He was buried in a tomb, raised from the dead on the third day, and after forty days of further ministry he subsequently ascended into the real Holy of Holies. *And there, for the first time in the entire history of redemption, a priest sat down.* Why? Because, praise be to God, purification *had been achieved.* Because the work of cleansing had, once and for all time, been accomplished—a sacrifice sufficient for the vilest of your sins and mine. As evidenced by what irrefutable act? *This priest sat down.*

And where, by the way, did he sit? "*At the right hand of the Majesty on high*" (Heb. 1:3). In the ancient world the right hand of a monarch was the place of supreme majesty and sovereignty. It is the place that this Son—the Word by whom God has now spoken to us—occupies. He is the cosmic Lord, the incarnate God, and our priestly King.

Now, you say, "OK. I've heard you. I've listened to what you've said. But does *any* of this have *any* bearing on *my* life?"

It *all* has *everything* to do with *your* life. Let me explain. When I was a young boy, my favorite week of the year was the one I spent at church camp. Even after all these years I can still remember the routine. Following the Sunday morning worship service, dozens of enthusiastic campers would pile into buses to make the three-hour drive into the Santa Cruz mountains. Having arrived, each of us would find our assigned cabins, claim our respective bunk bed, and then we would all gather on the baseball field for a group picture. We were told to squeeze together as closely as possible by a man standing very near the top of a tall ladder some fifty feet away. With a bullhorn he would instruct us to remain still, look straight at his camera, and smile. At just the right moment he snapped the picture.

At the end of the week, as we were nearing the time to leave, each camper was given a cylindrical tube made of cardboard with a lid covering the open end. It contained the group picture taken at the beginning of the week. Every year I did exactly same thing: I popped off the lid, pulled out the picture inside, unrolled it . . . and can you guess whose face I *always* looked for first?

"*Your own!*" you say. And, of course, you're absolutely right.

But how did *you* know I always looked for myself first? Because *you* are just as self-centered as I am! Because *you* always look for *yourself* first, don't you? But, my friend, contrary to your natural instinct, you are *not* the center of the universe. Nor am I the center of the universe. What we have seen from Hebrews is that the *Son of God* is the center of the universe. And the fact is, you will never know your place in this universe until you see yourself in proper alignment to him.

What does Hebrews 1:1–3 have to do with you? It has *everything* to do with you. *The Son of God is the cosmic Lord.* He made you. In a very real sense, you are already his, whether or not you presently acknowledge him. Your existence and eternal destiny are in his hands.

The Son of God is the incarnate God. In him, your search for God can end in success. To walk away from him in any direction is to court disaster.

The Son of God is the priestly King. In him, you can be free of all your sin and guilt. The fact is, you would be foolish to ignore him. After all, he is the King to whom every person ultimately bows, either in the present or in eternity, either in joyful allegiance or in guilty terror.

Don't turn away from God's Son. Don't walk away from God's Son. All of your hope for life and eternity resides in God's Son. *Come* to God's Son. If you've come to him before, then come to him once again—along with me—right now. If you've never come to God's Son, then come to him now. He'll not turn you away. He *will* receive you. I know that because this cosmic Lord . . . this incarnate God . . . this priestly King . . . is also the friend of sinners. And that includes you, just as it includes me.

Whatever you are enduring this morning—whatever your circumstances may be—stake your confidence in this: God is not silent. To the contrary, he has spoken *to you* in these last days. And his Word to you is his Son, Jesus Christ. Embrace him. Surrender to him. Trust in him.

He is better than everything . . . and everyone.